SEQUENTIAL MATHEMATICS
COURSE 1

JOHN ALLASIO
ANTHONY NIGRO
KATHLEEN THIBODEAU

Copyright © 1997 John Allasio, Anthony Nigro, Kathleen Thibodeau

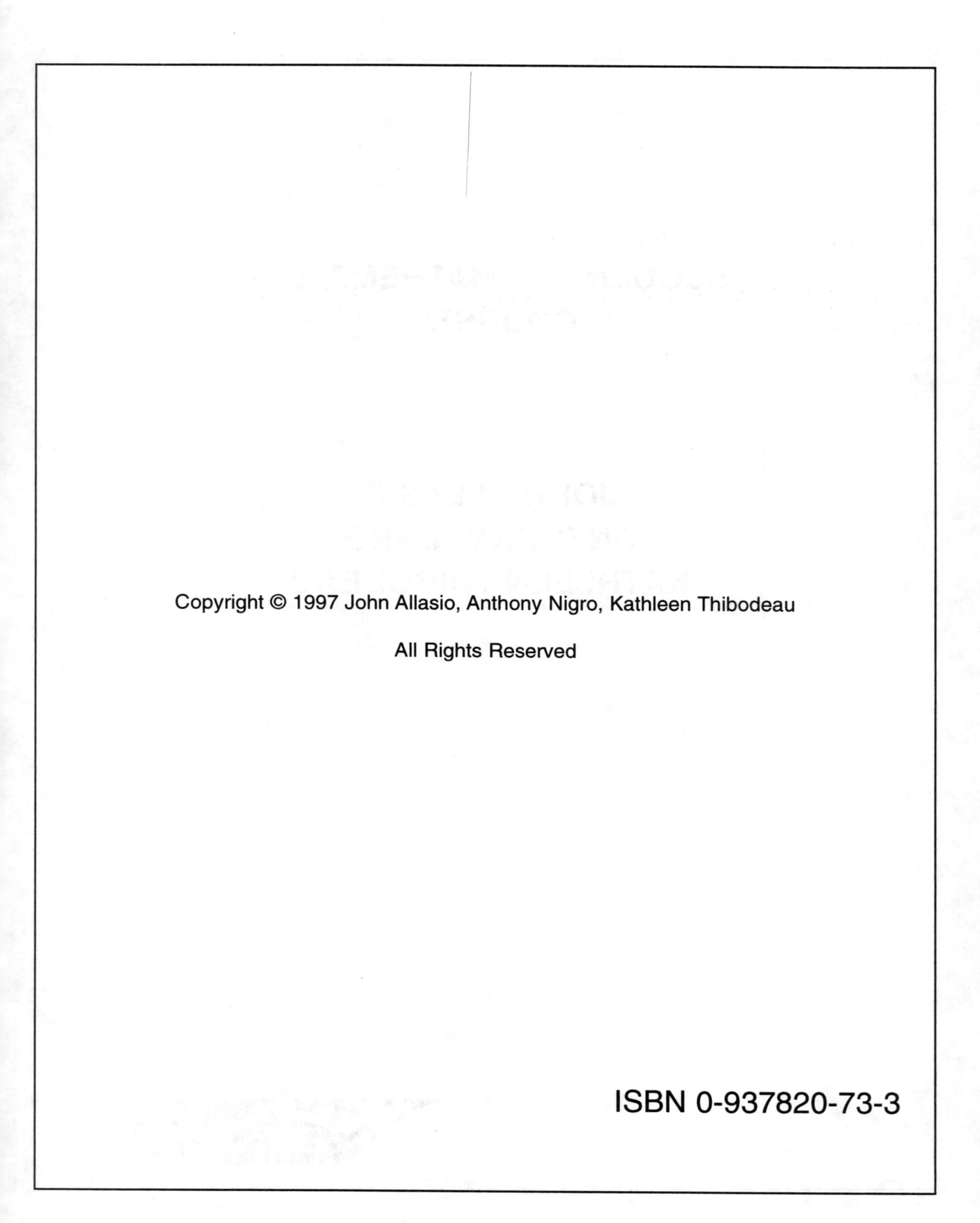

All Rights Reserved

ISBN 0-937820-73-3

INTRODUCTION

To meet the higher standards set by the New York State Board of Regents, the Sequential Math 1 Regents Exam Workbook has been revised. This updated version will provide an increased number of students with an invaluable tool to learn and/or to review the topics for the Regents in Sequential Math 1.

This revised regents review guide will provide extensive coverage of the New York State Curriculum for Sequential Math 1 through helpful reminders and multiple examples for each topic. Since the emphasis is on preparation for the Sequential Math 1 Regents, the examples are written in the same format and at the same level of difficulty as the regents exam.

This workbook was designed by experienced classroom teachers to give students the skills, knowledge and confidence necessary for them to pass the Regents in Sequential Math 1.

The student who uses this review workbook will be prepared to meet the challenge of the higher standards that are expected of all high school students.

SEQUENTIAL MATHEMATICS COURSE I
TABLE OF CONTENTS

CHAPTER 1   LOGIC

Negations 2
Conjunctions 3
Disjunctions 4
Conditionals 5
Biconditionals 6
Converse, Inverse, and Contrapositive 7
Combination Problems 8
CHAPTER TEST 9-10

CHAPTER 2   BASIC OF ALGEBRA

Signed Numbers 11
Order of Operations 12
Evaluating Expressions 13
Negative Exponents 14
Changing Units 15
Scientific Notation 16
Algebraic Expressions 17
Algebraic Expressions-Mixed 18
Percent Problems 19-21
CHAPTER TEST 22-23

CHAPTER 3 OPERATIONS IN ALGEBRA

Addition of Monomials and Polynomials 24
Subtraction of Monomials and Polynomials 25
Multiplication of Monomials 26
Multiplication of Polynomials by a Monomial 27
Multiplication of Binomials 28
Division of Monomials and Polynomials 29
Undefined Fractions 30
Addition and Subtraction of Fractions 31
Simplifying Radicals 32
Addition and Subtraction of Radicals 33
Mixed Operations 34
Factoring-Greatest Common Factor 35
Factoring-Difference between Two Perfect Squares 36
Factoring-General Trinomials 37
Factoring-Mixed 38
CHAPTER TEST 39-40

TABLE OF CONTENTS (CONTINUED)

CHAPTER 4   EQUATIONS and INEQUALITIES

Solving Equations 41
Solving Equations Containing Parenthesis 42
Solving Fractional Equations 43-44
Solving Decimal Equations 45
Solving Literal Equations 46
Solving Inequalities 47
One Variable Inequalities 48-49
Direct Variation 50
Number and Consecutive Integer Problems 51
Solving Simple Systems of Equations 52
Mixed Problems 53
CHAPTER TEST 54-55

CHAPTER 5   ANGLES AND TRIANGLES

Complementary and Supplementary Angles 56
Vertical Angles 57
Alternate Interior Angles 58
Corresponding Angles 59
Interior Angles on the Same Side of the Transversal 60
Angles and the Triangle 61
Special Kinds of Triangles 62-63
Pythagorean Theorem 64
Similarity 65
CHAPTER TEST 66-67

CHAPTER 6   GEOMETRIC CONCEPTS

Perimeter and Area 68-70
Parallelograms 71
Volume 72
The Circumference and Area of a Circle 73
Finding the Slope of a Line passing through two points 74
Equation of a Line 75
Equations of Special Lines 76
Points on a Line 77
Coordinate Geometry 78
Graphs of Inequalities 79
CHAPTER TEST 80-81

TABLE OF CONTENTS (CONTINUED)

CHAPTER 7 PROBABILITY AND STATISTICS

Counting Principle 82
Factorial and Permutations 83
Simple Probability 84
P (certain event), P(impossible event, Sample Space 85
Events A and B 86
Events A or B 87
Mode, Mean, Median 88
Quartiles and Percentiles 89
Mixed Problems 90
CHAPTER TEST 91-92

CHAPTER 8 TRANSFORMATIONS

Line Reflections 93
Translations 94
Rotations 95
Dilations 96
Line and Point Symmetry 97
CHAPTER TEST 98

REGENTS REVIEW   PART II

Tautologies 100-102
Pythagorean Theorem 103-104
Number Problems 105-107
Consecutive Integer Problems 108-109
Verbal Inequality Problems 110-111
Graphing Systems of Linear Equations in Two Variables 112-113
Algebraic Solution of a System of Linear Equations 114-115
Problem Solving 116-117
Graphing Systems of Inequalities 118-120
Perimeters of Polygons 121-123
Areas of Polygons 124-125
Area and Circumference of the circle 126-127
Areas of Polygons 128-129
Probability 130-133
Transformations 134-135
Quartiles and Percentiles 136-137
Frequency Histograms 138-140
Cumulative Frequency Histograms 141-144
PRACTICE REGENTS EXAMINATION 146-151

SEQUENTIAL MATHEMATICS COURSE 1

REGENTS REVIEW

PART I

Chapter 1
LOGIC

Negations

> **REMEMBER**
> A sentence that has a truth value is called a statement. A statement can be either True or False and by placing a "not" in the statement you have negated it. The negation of "John is in school" is "John is not in school." If we let p represent "John is in school" then the negation in symbolic form would be like this: ~ p

1. Write the negation of the statement: "A triangle has three sides".

2. The negation of a false statement is always
   (1) True
   (2) False
   (3) Neither true nor false
   (4) Cannot be determined

3. In symbolic form the negation of ~ p is equivalent to
   (1) ~p
   (2) q
   (3) p
   (4) ~(~(~p))

4. Is the negation of "8 + 7 ≠ 15" a true statement or a false statement?

5. Write in words the negation of "Tony knows how to ride a bicycle."

6. What would ~ (~ (~q)) be equivalent to?
   (1) q
   (2) ~(~q)
   (3) p
   (4) ~q

7. ~ (~p) is always equivalent to
   (1) ~p
   (2) q
   (3) ~(~(~(~p)))
   (4) none of the above

8. If r represents "the test was easy" then the symbolic form of "it is not true that the test was not easy" is
   (1) ~r
   (2) ~(~r)
   (3) ~(~(~r))
   (4) none of the above

9. Write in words the negation of "April is not a month of the year."

10. What would ~(~(~(~p))) be equivalent to?
    (1) p
    (2) ~p
    (3) q
    (4) ~(~(~p))

2

Chapter 1
LOGIC

Conjunctions

REMEMBER

A conjunction is a compound sentence formed by combining two simple sentences with the word "and". If p represents one simple sentence and q represents the other sentence then the symbolic form of "p and q" is

$$p \wedge q$$

When the sentence p and the sentence q take on different truth values then the conjunction "$p \wedge q$" has certain truth values as described in the truth table below.

p	q	p∧q
T	T	T
T	F	F
F	T	F
F	F	F

1. If p represents "8 + 2 = 10" and q represents "5 + 6 = 11", write the compound sentence "8 + 2 = 10" and "5 + 6 = 11" in symbolic form.

2. If r represents a true statement and q represents a false statement, what is the truth value of $r \wedge q$?

3. If r is true and q is true, what is the truth value of $\sim r \wedge q$?

4. What is the truth value of the conjunction "(9+2)=11 $\wedge$ (9+3) ≠ 11"?

5. Let p represent the statement "x is an odd number" and let q represent the statement "x > 8". If x = 7, which statement is true?
   (1) p∧q   (3) q
   (2) ~p   (4) p∧ ~q

6. If q represents "It is raining" and r represents "The sun is shining", write "It is raining and the sun is not shining" in symbolic form.

7. If r represents a false statement and q represents a true statement then what is the truth value of $\sim(r \wedge q)$?

8. If the truth value of $p \wedge q$ is true then?
   (1) p and q must both be true
   (2) p can be true and q can be false
   (3) p and q must both be false
   (4) none of the above

9. What is the value of x that would make the following conjunction true?
   $(4 + x = 6) \wedge (2 + 3 \neq 6)$

10. Let p represent the statement that "x is an even number" and let q represent the statement "x > 2". If x = 9, which statement is true?
    (1) p∧q   (3) q∧ ~p
    (2) p∧ ~q   (4) ~q

Chapter 1
LOGIC

Disjunctions

REMEMBER

A disjunction is a compound sentence formed by combining two simple sentences with the word "or". If p represents one simple sentence and q the other, then the symbolic form of "p or q" can be written as

$$p \vee q$$

The truth table for the disjunction is described below:

p	q	p ∨ q
T	T	T
T	F	T
F	T	T

1. If m represents "Today is Monday" and w represents "It is a washday", write the sentence "Today is Monday or it is a wash day" in symbolic form.

    _____

2. If p is true and q is true, what is the truth value of ~p ∨ ~q?

    _____

3. If s represents "Kay will study", write the sentence "Kay will study or will not study" in symbolic form.

    _____

4. If p represents "5 + 2 = 7" and q represents "x + 3 = 4", write "5 + 2 = 7 or x + 3 ≠ 4" in symbolic form.

    _____

5. Given that p is true, q is true and r is false, find the truth value of (p ∨ q) ∨ r.

    _____

6. If p is true and q is false, what is the truth value of ~(p ∨ q)?

    _____

7. If m represents "Marge likes logic" and j represents "John likes logic", write the sentence "Marge or John like logic" in symbolic form.

    _____

8. If p is true and q is false, what is the truth value of the following statement?
   (p ∨ q) ∧ ~q

    _____

9. When (p ∨ ~q) is false, then

    p is _____

    and

    q is _____

10. Given that p is true and both q and r are false, find the truth value of
    (p ∧ ~q) ∨ (q ∧ ~r).

    _____

4

Chapter 1
LOGIC

Conditionals

REMEMBER

"If it is raining then it is cloudy" is called a conditional sentence. If we let p represent "it is raining" and q represent "it is cloudy", then the original statement can be written in symbolic form as

$$p \rightarrow q$$

The truth table for the conditional is:

p	q	p → q
T	T	T
T	F	F
F	T	T
F	F	T

1. If r represents "it is Tuesday" and j represents "I am in school", write the sentence "If it is Tuesday, then I am in school" in symbolic form.

   _____

2. If p represents a true statement and q represents a false statement, which sentence is always false?
   (1) p → q   (3) p ∨ ~p
   (2) q → p   (4) ~p → q

   _____

3. If p is true and q is false, find the truth value of ~(q → p).

   _____

4. If p → q is a false statement, then

   p must always be _____

   and

   q must be _____

5. Let p represent the statement "x is even" and q represent "x ≤ 12". Which is true if x = 20?
   (1) p ∧ q   (3) ~p ∨ q
   (2) p → q   (4) p ∧ ~q

   _____

6. If p → q is false, then what is the truth value of p ∨ ~q?

   _____

7. If p represents "I am hungry" and q represents "I want a sandwich", write the sentence "If I am not hungry, then I don't want a sandwich" in symbolic form. _____

8. If p represents "5 + 1 = 6" and q represents "4 + 1 = 6", what is the truth value of p → q?

   _____

9. If p represents "8 > 6" and q represents "6 < 5", what is the truth value of q → p?

   _____

10. If p is true, q is false and r is false, what is the truth value of (p ∧ q) → ~r?

    _____

11. If p represents "It will snow" and q represents "We go to the dance", the statement "If we do not go to the dance, then it will snow" can be expressed by
    (1) p → q   (3) ~q → p
    (2) q → ~p   (4) ~p → ~q _____

5

Chapter 1
LOGIC

Biconditionals

REMEMBER

If you switch the order of p and q in the conditional p → q, you get the conditional q → p. A biconditional is formed by combining the conditionals p → q and q → p with an "and". In symbolic form the biconditional form would be (p → q) ∧ (q → p). A simple way to write the biconditional is

$$p \leftrightarrow q$$

and it is read as "p if and only if q". The truth table for the biconditional is described below.

p	q	p ↔ q
T	T	T
T	F	F
F	T	F
F	F	T

1. The expression r if and only if t can be written as
   (1) r → t   (3) r ↔ t
   (2) r ∨ t   (4) r ∧ t

2. If p is false and q is true, what is the truth value of q ↔ p?

3. If p represents "it is dark outside" and q represents "it is daytime", write in symbolic form the statement "it is dark outside if and only if it is daytime".

4. If p is true and q is false, what is the truth value of q ↔ ~p?

5. Which of the following is true when p is false and q is true?
   (1) p ↔ q   (3) p ∧ q
   (2) p → q   (4) ~(~(~q))

6. If p → q is false, what is the truth value of p ↔ q?

7. Let h represent "you're on the honor roll" and let n represent "your average is above 90%". Which is the symbolic representation of the statement "You are not on the honor roll if and only if your average is not above 90"?
   (1) ~h ∧ ~n   (3) n → h
   (2) ~n ↔ ~h   (4) ~h ↔ ~n

8. If p is true, q is false and r is true, find the truth value of the following statement:
   $$(p \leftrightarrow q) \land r$$

9. If p is true, q is true and r is false, find the truth value of the following statement:
   $$(\sim r \leftrightarrow q) \lor \sim p$$

Chapter 1
LOGIC

Converse, Inverse and the Contrapositive

REMEMBER

If you reverse the order of p and q in the conditional p → q, you get q → p.
q → p is called the converse of p → q

If you negate p and q in the conditional p → q, you get ~p → ~q.
~p → ~q is called the inverse of p → q

If you both negate and reverse the order of p and q in the conditional p → q, you get ~q → ~p.
~q → ~p is called the contrapositive of p → q

Important Note: If a conditional (p → q) is true, the converse and inverse do not necessarily have to be true, but the contrapositive will always be true.

---

1. Write in symbolic form, the converse of r → t.

2. Write in symbolic form, the inverse of q → t.

3. Write in symbolic form, the inverse of p → ~q.

4. Write in symbolic form, the contrapositive of q → p.

5. Which statement represents the inverse of the statement "If I do not practice, then I will lose the game"?
   (1) If I practice, then I will not lose the game.
   (2) If I lose the game, then I did not practice.
   (3) If I practice, then I will lose the game.
   (4) If I do not lose the game, then I did practice.

6. Which is logically equivalent to p → q?
   (1) ~q → p   (3) q → ~p
   (2) q → p   (4) ~q → ~p

7. If p → q is true, then ~q → ~p is
   (1) sometimes true   (3) always true
   (2) never true   (4) truth value cannot be determined

8. Write out in words, the converse of "If it's raining then it's cloudy".

9. Write out in words, the contrapositive of "If I passed the Sequential Math I exam, then I achieved a grade of 65% or better".

10. If a conditional sentence is true, then its converse must also be true.
    (Yes or No)

11. Which is logically equivalent to p → ~q?
    (1) ~q → p   (3) q → ~p
    (2) ~q → ~p   (4) ~p → q

Chapter 1
LOGIC

Combination Problems

> **REMEMBER**
> If p represents "x is an odd number" and q represents "x is a multiple of 4", which statement is true when $x = 16$?
>
>   (1) $p \vee q$ (2) $p \wedge q$ (3) $\sim p \rightarrow \sim q$ (4) $p \leftrightarrow q$
>
> Since $x=16$ is <u>even</u>, $\sim p$ is true. Because 16 is a <u>multiple of 4</u>, q is true.
>
> $p \vee q$ is true $p \wedge q$ is false $\sim p \rightarrow \sim q$ is false $p \leftrightarrow q$ is false   <u>Ans.</u> (1)

1. Let p represent "x is prime", and let q represent "x is even". Which statement is true if $x = 2$?
   (1) $\sim p \wedge q$ (3) $\sim p \vee \sim q$
   (2) $p \leftrightarrow \sim q$ (4) $\sim p \rightarrow q$

2. If p and q represent true statements, which compound statement is also true?
   (1) $p \wedge \sim q$ (3) $p \rightarrow \sim q$
   (2) $p \leftrightarrow \sim q$ (4) $\sim p \vee q$

3. Which statement would be a correct heading for the last column of the table?

p	q	$\sim q$	?
T	T	F	F
T	F	T	T
F	T	F	F
F	F	T	F

   (1) $p \vee \sim q$
   (2) $q \rightarrow \sim q$
   (3) $p \leftrightarrow \sim q$
   (4) $p \wedge \sim q$

4. If p is false and q is false, which expression is true?
   (1) $p \leftrightarrow q$ (3) $p \wedge q$
   (2) $p \vee q$ (4) $\sim p \rightarrow q$

5. Which expression is true when p is true and q is true?
   (1) $p \wedge \sim q$ (3) $p \rightarrow \sim q$
   (2) $\sim(p \vee q)$ (4) $\sim q \rightarrow \sim p$

6. Which statement is *always* false?
   (1) $p \rightarrow \sim q$ (3) $\sim p \rightarrow q$
   (2) $p \leftrightarrow q$ (4) $\sim p \wedge p$

7. Let p represent: "It is snowing".
   Let q represent: "The ski slopes are open".
   Let r represent: "There will be a bus trip".
   Which statement could be used to represent "If it is snowing and the ski slopes are open, then there will be a bus trip"?
   (1) $p \vee (q \rightarrow r)$ (3) $(p \vee q) \rightarrow r$
   (2) $p \wedge (q \rightarrow r)$ (4) $(p \wedge q) \rightarrow r$

8. Which statement is false if r is false and s is true?
   (1) $r \rightarrow (r \wedge s)$ (3) $r \wedge (r \wedge s)$
   (2) $(r \wedge s) \rightarrow s$ (4) $r \leftrightarrow (r \wedge s)$

Chapter 1
LOGIC
Chapter Test

1. If q represents the statement "It is Tuesday", write the negation of q in words.

2. Let p represent "x is odd". Let q represent the statement: "$x \leq 13$". Which is true if $x = 19$?
   (1) $p \rightarrow q$
   (2) $p \wedge q$
   (3) $\sim p \vee q$
   (4) $p \wedge \sim q$

3. Which is always false?
   (1) $r \rightarrow t$
   (2) $\sim r \rightarrow \sim t$
   (3) $r \vee \sim r$
   (4) $r \wedge \sim r$

4. If $p \wedge q$ is a true statement, then:
   (1) p is true and q is false
   (2) p is false and q is true
   (3) both p and q are true
   (4) both p and q are false

5. Which is logically equivalent to $p \rightarrow q$?
   (1) $\sim q \rightarrow \sim p$
   (2) $\sim p \rightarrow \sim q$
   (3) $q \rightarrow p$
   (4) $p \wedge \sim q$

6. If p represents "It is warm" and q represents "It is winter", write in symbolic form the statement: "If it is winter then it is not warm".

7. The inverse of $p \rightarrow \sim q$ is
   (1) $\sim p \rightarrow \sim q$
   (2) $\sim p \rightarrow q$
   (3) $\sim q \rightarrow p$
   (4) $q \rightarrow \sim p$

8. Write in words, the negation of "June is not a month of the year".

9. Let p represent "$x = 6$" and q represent "$x + 2 = 8$". Using p and q, write in symbolic form:
   "$x = 6$ if and only if $x + 2 = 8$"

10. Let p represent "$x \geq 8$" and let q represent the statement "$3x = 15$". Which is true for $x = 10$?
    (1) $p \wedge q$
    (2) $p \vee q$
    (3) $p \rightarrow q$
    (4) $p \leftrightarrow q$

11. If *p* represents "It will rain" and *q* represents "we go to the movies", the statement "If we go to the movies, then it will not rain" can be expressed by
    (1) $p \rightarrow q$
    (2) $q \rightarrow \sim p$
    (3) $\sim q \rightarrow p$
    (4) $\sim p \rightarrow \sim q$

Chapter 1
LOGIC
Chapter Test (Continued)

12. Which statement is false when q is false and r is false?
    (1) q → r (3) ~q → ~r
    (2) q ∧ r (4) q ↔ r
    _____

13. The inverse of ~p → ~q is
    (1) ~q → ~p (3) q → p
    (2) ~q → p   (4) p → q
    _____

14. Let p represent "I will study" and let q represent "I will go shopping". Using p and q, write in symbolic form, "I will study or I will not go shopping".
    _____

15. Write in symbolic form the contrapositive of R → ~S.
    _____

16. If p is false and q is true, find the truth value of the statement: (p ∨ q) ∧ (~p → q)
    _____

17. Let p represent "The number is an odd number" and let q represent "The number is divisible by 2". Write in symbolic form "If a number is divisible by 2, then it is not an odd number".
    _____

18. Write in symbolic form using s and t, the converse of ~s → ~t.
    _____

19. Which statement represents the converse of the statement "If I do not study, then I will fail"?
    (1) If I study, then I will not fail
    (2) If I fail, then I did not study
    (3) If I study, then I will fail
    _____

20. If p is true and q is false, find the truth value of the statement:
    [(p → q) ∧ ~p] → ~q
    _____

21. Which of the following is true when p is false and q is false?
    (1) p ∨ q   (3) ~(~p)
    (2) p ∧ q   (4) p ↔ q
    _____

22. Let a represent the statement "The sun is shining" and let b represent the statement "It is hot". Write in symbolic form the converse of the statement using a and b, "If it is not hot, the sun is shining".
    _____

23. If a conditional statement is false, the inverse of the converse of that statement is always true. (Answer True or False)
    _____

24. If p represents "x is an even number" and q represents "x is a multiple of 7", which statement is true when x = 49?
    (1) p ∨ q (2) p ∧ q (3) ~p → ~q (4) p ↔ q
    _____

25. Let p represent "x is an odd integer", and let q represent "x is a multiple of 3". For which value of x will p ∧ q be true?
    (1) 1 (2) 6 (3) 9 (4) 12
    _____

10

Chapter 2
BASICS OF ALGEBRA

Signed Numbers

> **REMEMBER**
>
> **Addition of signed numbers**--If the signs are the same, keep the sign and add the numbers. If the signs are different, use the sign of the larger number and subtract the numbers.
>
> **Subtraction of signed numbers**--Change the sign of the bottom number and follow the same rules as in addition of signed numbers.
>
> **Multiplication of signed numbers**--If there is an even amount of negative signs, the answer will be positive. If there is an odd amount of negative signs, the answer will be negative.
>
> **Division of signed numbers**--If the signs are the same, the answer will be positive. If the signs are different, the answer will be negative.

1. Add:

    (a) - 5   (b) -12   (c) -13
        + 9   + 8   - 6

2. Subtract:

    (a) -15   (b) + 6   (c) -11
        + 5   - 8   - 3

3. Multiply:

    (a) - 8   (b) + 6   (c) -12
        - 9   - 7   + 4

4. Divide:

    (a) $\frac{-24}{+8}$ = _____   (b) $\frac{-18}{-9}$ = _____   (c) $\frac{20}{-4}$ = _____

5. Find the sum of -23 and -18.

6. Find the product of -30 and 6.

7. Find the difference of 10 and -6.

8. Find the quotient of -40 and -8.

9. Subtract -6 from -8.

10. Simplify: (+8) - (-6) + (-12).

Chapter 2
BASICS OF ALGEBRA

Order of Operations

REMEMBER

Evaluate all powers first. Then do all multiplications and/or divisions as they appear from left to right. Then do all additions and/or subtractions as they appear from left to right. If there are any grouping symbols, start the operations with the innermost set of grouping symbols.

Examples:
$$6 + 2^3 \div 2 - 3$$
$$6 + 8 \div 2 - 3$$
$$6 + 4 - 3$$
$$10 - 3$$
$$7$$

$$9(3+2) + 3(10 \div 5)$$
$$9(5) + 3(2)$$
$$45 + 6$$
$$51$$

1. Evaluate: $9 - 6 \div 3 + 8$

2. Evaluate: $4(3) + 20 \div 5$

3. Find the value of:
$3^3 + 2^2(3) - 8$

4. Evaluate: $3(9 - 2) + 14 \div 7$

5. Simplify:
$8 - 2(3)^2$

6. Evaluate:
$4(3^2 - 2^3)^4$

7. Find the value of:
$3(2)(4) - 12 \div 6(3)$

8. Evaluate:
$[(4 \cdot 8 - 2) \div 5] \div 3$

9. Evaluate:
$4^2 \div 8 + 4^3 - 6(3)$

10. Evaluate:
$27 - 3 + 12 \div 4 \div 3$

11. Simplify:
$5(9) - [3 + 5(2)^2]$

12. Find the value of:
$12 \div 3(2) + 5$

Chapter 2
BASICS OF ALGEBRA
Evaluating Expressions

REMEMBER
Replace the letters with the number values and follow the order of operations.

Example: If $a = 2$ and $b = -3$, find the value of $(a + b)^2$
$(a + b)^2 = (2 + (-3))^2 = (-1)^2 = 1$

1. Find the value of $4x^2y$ if $x = -3$ and $y = 2$.

2. If $x = 2$ and $y = -1$, which expression has a value of 5?
   (1) $x^2 + y$ (3) $x + 3y$
   (2) $x^2 - y$ (4) $x^2 + 2y$

3. Find the value of the expression $5x^3$ when $x = -2$.
   (1) -30   (3) -40
   (2) +30   (4) +40

4. Given the formula $A = \frac{1}{2}bh$, find the value of A if $b = 5$ and $h = 8$.

5. If $x = 8$ and $y = 3$, find the value of $\frac{4}{x} - \frac{1}{y}$.

6. What is the value of $6xy^2$ when $x = 2$ and $y = -3$?
   (1) -108   (3) +72
   (2) +108   (4) -72

7. Find C in $C = \frac{5}{9}(F - 32)$ if $F = 14$.
   (1) 10   (3) 25
   (2) -10   (4) 100

8. If $x = 6$ and $y = 5$, find the value of $\frac{x}{8} + \frac{2}{y}$.

9. If $x = -4$ and $y = 2$, which expression has a value of 12?
   (1) $x^2 + y^2$ (3) $2x + 2y$
   (2) $x^2 - y^2$ (4) $2x - 2y$

10. Find the value of $-2x^3$ if $x = -3$.

Chapter 2
BASICS OF ALGEBRA

Negative Exponents

REMEMBER
To change a negative exponent to a positive exponent, take the reciprocal of the expression and use the positive exponent.

Examples: $2^{-5} = \frac{1}{2^5}$ $\frac{1}{x^{-3}} = x^3$ $\frac{a^{-4}}{b^{-2}} = \frac{b^2}{a^4}$ $a^2b^{-5} = \frac{a^2}{b^5}$

---

1. The value of 3^{-3} is

   (1) 27 (3) $\frac{1}{27}$
   (2) $\frac{1}{9}$ (4) 9

   _____

2. Write as an expression with positive exponents:
   $$5a^{-3}b^{-2}c$$

   _____

3. Write the fraction $\frac{1}{8}$ as a whole number with a negative exponent.

   _____

4. Write with positive exponents only:
   $$a^{-5}b^4$$

   _____

5. Find the value of: $16\,(2)^{-4}$

   _____

6. Find the equivalent of $\frac{5^{-2}}{3^{-2}}$

   (1) $\frac{3^{-2}}{5^{-2}}$ (3) $(5^2)(3^2)$
   (2) 15^2 (4) $\frac{3^2}{5^2}$

   _____

7. Find the value of: $2\left(\frac{1}{4}\right)^{-2}$

   (1) 32 (3) $\frac{1}{8}$
   (2) 16 (4) 4

   _____

8. Write with only positive exponents:
   $$3a^{-2}b^{-3}$$

   _____

9. Evaluate: $8^2 \div \frac{1}{2^{-4}}$

   _____

10. Find the value of: 4^{-3}

    (1) -12 (3) 64
    (2) $\frac{1}{64}$ (4) $\frac{1}{12}$

    _____

Chapter 2
BASICS OF ALGEBRA

Changing Units

> **REMEMBER**
> When changing larger units to smaller units, multiply. When changing smaller units to larger units, divide.
> **Example:** Change 3.2 meters to centimeters.
> **Solution:** Since there are 100 centimeters in one meter, and meters are larger than centimeters, multiply 3.2 x 100 which equals 320 cm. ans.

1. Change 4.6 km to meters.
    (1) 460m   (3) 46m
    (2) 4600m   (4) .046 m

2. Express the number of months in d years.
    (1) 12d   (3) d + 12
    (2) $\frac{d}{12}$ (4) d - 12

3. Expressed as meters per minute, 30 km/hr is equal to:
    (1) 1.8m/min   (3) 50 m/min
    (2) 18 m/min   (4) 500 m/min

4. How many weeks are there in x days?

5. Change y yards into inches.
    (1) 12y   (3) $\frac{y}{12}$
    (2) 36y   (4) $\frac{y}{36}$

6. Expressed as kilometers per hour, 1,000 m/min. is equivalent to:
    (1) 60 km/hr   (3) 600 km/hr
    (2) 6 km/hr   (4) 6,000 km/hr

7. Find the number of pounds in q ounces.
    (1) 16q   (3) $\frac{q}{16}$
    (2) 12q   (4) $\frac{q}{12}$

8. Change 3.27 cm to meters.
    (1) 327 m   (3) .0327 m
    (2) .327 m   (4) 32.7 m

9. How many quarts are there in 3 gallons 1 quart?

10. How many miles are there in 7,920 feet? (5,280 ft = 1 mile)

Chapter 2
BASICS OF ALGEBRA

Scientific Notation

> **REMEMBER**
>
> To express a number greater than one in scientific notation form, write it as a number between 1 and 10 multiplied by 10^n. The exponent n can be found by counting the number of decimal places to the right of the decimal point.
>
> **Example:** Express 280,000 in scientific notation form.
> **Solution:** $280,000 = 2.8 \times 10^5$ Ans.
>
> To express a number less than one in scientific notation form, write it as a number between 1 and 10 multiplied by 10^n. The exponent -n can be found by counting the number of decimal places to the left of the decimal point.
>
> **Example:** Express 0.0032 in scientific notation form.
> **Solution:** $0.0032 = 3.2 \times 10^{-3}$ Ans.

1. If 580,000 is expressed in the form of 5.8×10^n, what is the value of n?

2. If 0.000076 is expressed in the form 7.6×10^n, what is the value of n?
   (1) -4   (3) 5
   (2) -5   (4) 4

3. Write the number 87,000,000 in scientific notation form.

4. Write the number 0.0094 in scientific notation form.

5. Written in standard notation, 6.1×10^4 is equivalent to:
   (1) 6,100   (3) .0061
   (2) .00061   (4) 61,000

6. Expressed in decimal form, the number 3.26×10^{-3} is:
   (1) .00326   (3) 3,260
   (2) .0326   (4) 32.600

7. If the number 0.000051 is written in the form 5.1×10^n, what is the value of n?

8. What is the value of n if the number 88,000 is written in the form 8.8×10^n?

16

Chapter 2
BASICS OF ALGEBRA

Algebraic Expressions

REMEMBER
Write the numbers and letters given in the current mathematical order of operations. If no letters are given in the problem, select any letter, such as x or y.

Example: Write an algebraic expression for "seven times the sum of x and y:.
Solution: 7 (x + y) Ans.

---

1. Write the algebraic expression for "nine times a number decreased by two".

2. Marge is three times as old as Mary. If x represents Mary's age, which expression represents how old Marge will be in five years?

    (1) 3x + 5   (3) 3x - 5
    (2) 3 (x + 5)   (4) 3 (x - 5)

3. Using the letter y to represent a number, express "eight less than six times this number" in terms of y.

4. If three boxes of raisins cost x dimes, what is the cost in cents, of one box?

    (1) $\frac{x}{3}$ (3) 3x
    (2) $\frac{3}{10x}$ (4) $\frac{10x}{3}$

5. Expressed in terms of y, the number of months in y years is:

    (1) $\frac{12}{y}$ (3) $\frac{y}{12}$
    (2) 12y   (4) 52y

6. If two numbers add up to 11 and one of the numbers is x, what is the other number?

7. Which expression represents "ten divided by x plus 2".

    (1) $\frac{10}{x+2}$ (3) $\frac{x}{10} + 2$
    (2) $\frac{10}{x} + 2$ (4) $\frac{x+2}{10}$

8. Expressed in terms of m, the number of hours m minutes is:

    (1) $\frac{60}{m}$ (3) 12m
    (2) 60m   (4) $\frac{m}{60}$

Chapter 2
BASICS OF ALGEBRA

Algebraic Expressions - Mixed

1. Which is the additive inverse of $\frac{-5}{x}$?
   (1) $\frac{x}{5}$
   (2) $\frac{-x}{5}$
   (3) $\frac{5}{x}$
   (4) 0

2. The area of a triangle is equal to $\frac{1}{2}$ the product of the base times the altitude. If both the base and the altitude are doubled, the area will:
   (1) remain the same
   (2) double
   (3) be multiplied by 4
   (4) triple

3. The product of $\frac{1}{x}$, $x \neq 0$, and its reciprocal will be:
   (1) 1
   (2) -1
   (3) x
   (4) -x

4. If x = 4 then the value of $\sqrt{x-8}$ is:
   (1) a rational number
   (2) an irrational number
   (3) imaginary
   (4) an integer

5. Which sentence illustrates the distributive property for addition?
   (1) a + 0 = 0
   (2) a + b = b + a
   (3) (a + b) + c = a + (b + c)
   (4) a(b + c) = ab + ac

6. Which is a rational number?
   (1) $\sqrt{17}$
   (2) π
   (3) $\sqrt{-16}$
   (4) $\sqrt{0.25}$

7. Which sentence illustrates the reflexive property?
   (1) a(b · c) = (a · b)c
   (2) ab = ab
   (3) ab = ba
   (4) a(b + c) = ab + ac

8. The volume of a rectangular solid is equal to the product of the length times the width times the height. If the length, width and height are all cut in half, the volume will be:
   (1) multiplied by $\frac{1}{2}$
   (2) multiplied by $\frac{1}{8}$
   (3) multiplied by 4
   (4) multiplied by 8

9. a + (b + c) = (a + b) + c illustrates which property?
   (1) Commutative
   (2) Distributive
   (3) Associative
   (4) Reflexive

10. The multiplicative inverse of -3 is:
    (1) 0
    (2) $-\frac{1}{3}$
    (3) +3
    (4) $\frac{1}{3}$

Chapter 2
BASICS OF ALGEBRA

Percent Problems

> **REMEMBER**
> Case 1 - To find the percent of a number, change the percent to a decimal and multiply.
>
> **Example:** What is twelve percent of thirty-six?
>
> 12% = .12
>
> ```
>      36
>    x .12
>      72
>     36
>    4.32  ans.
> ```

1. If the sales tax rate is 8%, what is the amount of sales tax which must be paid on a $250 T.V. set?

2. What is 15% of 60?
   (1) 400 (3) 90
   (2) 25   (4) 9

3. Find 11% of 22.

4. What is 12.6% of 50?

5. If the discount rate is 20%, what is the amount of discount for a coat costing $150?

6. What is the sales tax on a watch costing $200 if the sales tax rate is 10%?
   (1) $20.00   (3) $220.00
   (2) $2.00   (4) $22.00

7. Find 25% of 25.

8. What is 9% of 45?

9. Find 40% of 320.

10. What is 6.3% of 80?

11. What is the discount on a radio originally priced at $90 with a discount rate of 15%?

Chapter 2
BASICS OF ALGEBRA

Percent Problems (Continued)

REMEMBER

Case II - To find the number when a percent of it is given, change the percent to a decimal and divide by the decimal.

Example: Twelve percent of what number is thirty-six?

$$12\% = .12 \qquad .12 \overline{)36.00} = 300 \text{ ans.}$$

---

1. Thirty percent of what number is 15?
   (1) 4.5   (3) 5
   (2) 2   (4) 50

2. Twenty-four is eight percent of what number?

3. Forty is twenty-five percent of what number?

4. Sixty percent of what number is eighteen?

5. Seven percent of what number is seven?
   (1) 1   (3) 10
   (2) 100   (4) 49

6. Fifteen is five percent of what number?
   (1) 300   (3) 3
   (2) 75   (4) 30

7. Two percent of what number is twenty-two?
   (1) 44   (3) 11
   (2) 1100 (4) 4400

8. Fifty-two is thirteen percent of what number?

9. Three percent of what number is six?

10. If 10% of a number is 4x, then the number is:
    (1) .4x   (3) 400x
    (2) 40x   (4) 4

Chapter 2
BASICS OF ALGEBRA

Percent Problems (Continued)

REMEMBER

Case III - To find what percent one number is of another number, divide placing the "is" number <u>inside</u> and the "of" number <u>outside</u>. Change the decimal to a percent.

Example: Twelve is what percent of thirty-six?

$$36 \overline{)12.00}^{.33\frac{12}{36}} = .33\frac{1}{3} = 33\frac{1}{3}\% \text{ ans.}$$

1. If Dave answered 15 out of 20 questions correctly, what percent of the questions did he answer correctly?
   (1) $\frac{3}{4}$%   (3) 3%
   (2) 75%   (4) $133\frac{1}{3}$%

2. What percent of 30 is 6?

3. Ten is what percent of forty-five?
   (1) 22%   (3) 4.5%
   (2) 450%   (4) $22\frac{2}{9}$%

4. What percent of 80 is 20?
   (1) 40%   (3) 25%
   (2) 400%   (4) 4%

5. What percent of nine is three?

6. Fourteen is what percent of twenty?
   (1) 70%   (3) $\frac{7}{10}$%
   (2) 7%   (4) 2.8%

7. What percent of 12 is 8?

8. Fifty is what percent of 100?
   (1) 50%   (3) 200%
   (2) 2%   (4) 5%

9. John made six out of eight foul shots in a basketball game. What percent of his shots did he make?
   (1) 25%   (3) 33%
   (2) 50%   (4) 75%

10. What percent of fifty-five is eleven?

Chapter 2
BASICS OF ALGEBRA
Chapter Test

1. Find the value of $6 + 4 \div (-1)$.
   - (1) 9
   - (2) 2
   - (3) 7
   - (4) 10

2. Which is an irrational number?
   - (1) $\frac{-4}{5}$
   - (2) 0
   - (3) $\sqrt{49}$
   - (4) π

3. Evaluate the expression $4x + 3y$ if $x = -1$ and $y = 2$.

4. Subtract -18 from -24.

5. The value of 7^{-3} is:
   - (1) -21
   - (2) $\frac{1}{343}$
   - (3) $\frac{1}{21}$
   - (4) 343

6. Change 540 meters to centimeters.

7. If the number 4,500,000 is written in the form 4.5×10^n, what is the value of n?

8. Which sentence illustrates the commutative property of addition?
   - (1) $ab = ba$
   - (2) $a(b+c) = ab + ac$
   - (3) $a + b = b + a$
   - (4) $ab = ab$

9. What is the sales tax on a radio costing $50 if the sales tax rate is 5%?
   - (1) $52.50
   - (2) $10
   - (3) $25.00
   - (4) $2.50

10. Evaluate:
    $$4^3 + 3^2 (2) + 1$$

11. Expressed in decimal form, the number 6.8×10^{-4} is:
    - (1) .00068
    - (2) 68,000
    - (3) .0068
    - (4) .068

12. Fifty-one is 17% of what number?

Chapter 2
BASICS OF ALGEBRA

Chapter Test (Continued)

13. Find the value of $-2x^4$ if $x = -2$.

14. John had three hits in a baseball game out of eight times at bat. What was his batting average?
    (1) .375   (3) $2.66\frac{2}{3}$
    (2) .38   (4) .400

15. Which is an imaginary number?
    (1) π (3) $\sqrt{37}$
    (2) $\sqrt{-1}$ (4) $\sqrt{81}$

16. How many days are there in w weeks?
    (1) 12w   (3) 365w
    (2) 52w   (4) 7w

17. Find the cost of a coat if there is a 25% discount on the original selling price of $160.
    (1) $40   (3) $200
    (2) $125   (4) $120

18. How many gallons are there in 18 quarts?

19. If $x = -3$ and $y = -1$, which expression has a value of -4?
    (1) $x^2 + 3y$ (3) $3x + 5y$
    (2) $2x^2 - 14y$ (4) $x + y^3$

20. Find the value of $3 + 9 \div 3 + 3$.
    (1) 7   (3) 9
    (2) 2   (4) 4.5

21. If the area of a square equals S^2, how would you make the area one-fourth the original size?
    (1) S is doubled   (3) S is divided by 4
    (2) S is tripled   (4) S is divided by 2

22. 300 is 15% of what number?

23. The value of $(-4)^{-2}$ is:
    (1) $\frac{1}{16}$ (3) -16
    (2) 16   (4) $\frac{1}{8}$

24. Express the number of meters in c centimeters.

Chapter 3
OPERATIONS IN ALGEBRA

Addition of Monomials and Polynomials

REMEMBER
In order to add monomials or polynomials, the terms must be similar.

Example:

$$8a^2$$
$$+4a^2$$
$$\overline{12a^2}$$

$$6x^3 - 2x + 8$$
$$3x^3 - 8x - 2$$
$$\overline{9x^3 - 10x + 6}$$

1. Find the sum of $6x^3$, $9x^3$ and $-4x^3$.

2. Add: $17a^3 - 19a - 3$
$16a^3 + 23a - 11$

3. Combine:
$(4a - 5b) + (2a - 8b) + (a + b)$

4. Find the sum of -13ab, -8ab and -5ab.
   (1) 26ab   (3) -26ab
   (2) ab   (4) 10ab

5. Find the total of $6x^2 - 3y^2$, $8x^2 + 7y^2$, and $2x^2 + 5y^2$.

6. Find the sum:
$(3x - 5y + 4) + (-5x - y - 1) + (-6x + 3y + 1)$

7. What is the sum of $8x + 7y$, $-12x + 3z$, and $-4y + 6z$?

8. Add: $-19R^2 + 7R - 6$
$-13R^2 - 8R + 6$

9. Express the sum of $24c^2 + 23c + 8$ and $31c^2 - 14c - 11$ as a trinomial.

10. Add: $-3x + 5y$, $-4x - 6y$, and $9x + 4y$.

11. Combine:
$(9y^2 + 7) + (3y^2 - 5) + (-2y^2 + 1)$

12. Find the sum:
$(-2a - 3b + 5) + (6a + 8b - 6) + (-a - b - 3)$

24

Chapter 3
OPERATIONS IN ALGEBRA
Subtraction of Monomials and Polynomials

REMEMBER
In order to subtract monomials or polynomials, the terms must be similar. Don't forget to change signs!

Examples: Subtract: $+6x^3$
                            $+-2x^3$
                            $8x^3$

$(8a^2 - 4) - (6a^2 + 6) =$
$8a^2 - 4 - 6a^2 - 6 =$
$2a^2 - 10$

1. Express as a trinomial:
   $(6x^2 + 3x - 2) - (3x^2 - 4x + 5)$

2. From $(4a^2 + a - 1)$ subtract $(a^2 - 3a + 4)$.

3. Combine:
   $(2a + b) - (a + b)$

4. Subtract: $-3x^2 + 5xy + 6y^2$
               $8x^2 + 9xy - 8y^2$

5. From $(-13x^2y^2)$ subtract $(-6x^2y^2)$.

6. Combine:
   $(-3x - 2y) - (2x + 3y)$

7. Subtract:
   $18b^2 + 6b - 7$
   $-3b^2 + 5b + 8$

8. Express as a trinomial:
   $(7c^2 - 6c - 5) - (2c^2 + 5c + 1)$

9. Subtract $(8x^2 + 6x + 3)$ from $(-2x^2 + 5x - 9)$.

10. Combine:
    $(3x + 2y) - (2x - 3y) - (x - y)$

Chapter 3
OPERATIONS IN ALGEBRA

Multiplication of Monomials

REMEMBER
If the bases are the same, add the exponents.

Example: The product of $6x^3$ and $5x^2 = (6)(5) x^{3+2} = 30x^5$

1. Find the product of $8x^2$ and $6x^2$.

2. Multiply: $-3ab$ by $-2a^2b$.

3. What does $7y^3$ times $-3y^4$ equal?
   (1) $-21y^7$ (3) $21y^{12}$
   (2) $-21y^{12}$ (4) $21y^7$

4. Multiply: xy by $4xy$.
   (1) $4x^2y^2$ (3) $4xy$
   (2) $5x^2y^2$ (4) $5xy$

5. Find the product of $-9a^4$ and $-3a^3$.

6. What is the product of $\frac{2}{3} xy$ and $\frac{9}{10} xy$?

7. What does $-6x^2$ times $3x^4$ equal?
   (1) $-18x^6$ (3) $18x^6$
   (2) $-18x^8$ (4) $18x^8$

8. Find the product of $10x$ and $10x$.

9. Multiply: $12x^2y$ by $3xy^2$.

10. What is the product of $\frac{1}{8} x^4y$ and $\frac{1}{2} xy^3$?

11. The expression $-4x(-4x^2)$ is equal to:
    (1) $-16x^3$ (3) $8x^3$
    (2) $16x^3$ (4) $16x^2$

12. The product $(-5x^2)(4x^3)$ is equal to:
    (1) $-20x^6$ (3) $-20x^5$
    (2) $20x^6$ (4) $20x^5$

Chapter 3
OPERATIONS IN ALGEBRA
Multiplication of Polynomials by a Monomial

REMEMBER
To multiply a polynomial by a monomial, multiply each term of the polynomial by the monomial.

Example: Multiply: $3x(4x + 6)$

$3x(4x + 6) = 12x^2 + 18x$

---

1. Multiply: $5x(7x - 3)$

2. Find the product: $7a(3a + b)$

3. Multiply: $2x(4x^2 - 7x + 2)$

4. The product of $8y(4y - 2)$ is:
   (1) $12y^2 - 16y$ (3) $32y^2 - 16y$
   (2) $32y - 16$ (4) $16y^2$

5. Multiply: $6x(5 - 2x)$
   (1) $30x - 12x^2$ (3) $30x - 8x^2$
   (2) $30x^2 - 12x$ (4) $30x^2 - 8x$

6. Multiply: $\frac{1}{2}x(4x + 6)$

7. What does $10(3x^2 + 2x - 1)$ equal?
   (1) $30x^2 + 20x - 1$ (3) $30x^2 + 20x + 10$
   (2) $30x^2 + 2x - 1$ (4) $30x^2 + 20x - 10$

8. Multiply: $12a(6a - 3)$

9. Find the product: $9(4x^2 + 3)$

10. Multiply: $4y(-4 + 4y)$

11. The product of $20(2 + 3x^2)$ is:
    (1) $40x + 60x^2$ (3) $40 + 60x^2$
    (2) $40 + 60x$ (4) $40x^2 + 60x$

12. Multiply: $\frac{1}{5}(10x^2 + 25x + 5)$

Chapter 3
OPERATIONS IN ALGEBRA

Multiplication of Binomials

REMEMBER

For the product of a binomial times a binomial, use the FOIL system. [First, Outer, Inner, Last]

Example: $(3x + 2)(2x + 1) = 6x^2 + 3x + 4x + 2$
$= 6x^2 + 7x + 2$

1. Express the product $(x + 3)(x - 2)$ as a trinomial.

2. Multiply $3a - 5$ by $7a - 3$.

3. Find the product of $4a + 5$ and $4a + 5$.

4. Express $(6x - 2)(3x - 1)$ as a trinomial.

5. What is the product of $2a + b$ and $2a - b$?

6. If $(4x - 5)(2x + 3)$ is written in the form $ax^2 + bx + c$, what is the value of b?

7. Simplify:
$(2x + 3)^2$

8. Find the product of $8x - 7y$ and $8x + 7y$.

9. Express the product $(10x - 3)(3x - 4)$ as a trinomial.

10. Multiply $5a - 7$ times $2a + 4$.

11. Express as a trinomial:
$(7a + 2b)(3a + 2b)$

12. If $(7x + 6)(11x - 8)$ is written in the form, $ax^2 + bx + c$, what is the value of c?

Chapter 3
OPERATIONS IN ALGEBRA
Division of Monomials and Polynomials

REMEMBER
If the bases are the same, subtract the exponents.

Examples: $12x^6 \div 2x^3 = 6x^3$ $\qquad \dfrac{25x^3 - 15x^2 + 5x}{5x} = 5x^2 - 3x + 1$

1. Find the quotient of $-18x^8$ and $2x^2$.

2. Divide:
$-36x^2 \div -9x^2$

3. Divide:
$(24x^3 - 18x^2 + 12x) \div 6x$

4. Divide:
$(30x^5 - 15x^3) \div 5x^2$

5. Find the quotient:
$\dfrac{72x^4 + 24x^3}{12x}$

6. Divide:
$48a^{12}$ by $\tfrac{2}{3}a^4$

7. Divide:
$14x^4 + 22x^3 - 18x^2$ by $2x^2$

8. Divide:
$-24x^{12}y^9$ by $3x^3$

9. Find the quotient of:
$\dfrac{42y^2 - 14y - 7}{7}$

10. Divide:
$(32x^4 + 16x^3 - 24x^2) \div 8x$

11. Divide:
$100a^5b^{15}$ by $-10a^5b^5$

12. Divide:
$63x^3 - 18x^2 + 9x$ by $9x$.

Chapter 3
OPERATIONS IN ALGEBRA

Undefined Fractions

> **REMEMBER**
> A fraction is considered undefined when it has a denominator with a value of zero.
>
> **Example:** $\frac{6}{x+2}$ is undefined when $x = -2$.

1. The expression $\frac{5}{x-2}$ is undefined for what value of x?
   (1) -2   (3) 0
   (2) +2   (4) 7

   _____

2. Which expression is undefined or meaningless when x = 4?
   (1) $\frac{1}{4x}$ (3) $\frac{1}{x-4}$
   (2) x^{-4} (4) $\frac{1}{x+4}$

   _____

3. For which value of x is the expression $\frac{x-6}{x+5}$ undefined?
   (1) -6   (3) 5
   (2) -5   (4) 6

   _____

4. Which is undefined when x = 3?
   (1) x - 3   (3) $\frac{x}{3}$
   (2) $\frac{1}{x-3}$ (4) x^0

   _____

5. For which value of x is the expression $\frac{x}{x-7}$ undefined?
   (1) 1   (3) 7
   (2) -7   (4) 0

   _____

6. Which is undefined when x = 1?
   (1) $\frac{x+1}{x}$ (3) $\frac{x}{x+1}$
   (2) $\frac{x-1}{x}$ (4) $\frac{x}{x-1}$

   _____

7. The expression $\frac{8}{x+9}$ is undefined for what value of x?
   (1) 9   (3) -8
   (2) 8   (4) -9

   _____

8. Which expression is undefined or meaningless when x = 5?
   (1) $\frac{x^2}{x-5}$ (3) $\frac{x^2}{x+5}$
   (2) $\frac{x^0}{x}$ (4) x-5

   _____

Chapter 3
OPERATIONS IN ALGEBRA

Addition & Subtraction of Fractions

REMEMBER
Both addition and subtraction of fractions are solved in the same way. Find the least common denominator and then combine like terms.

Example: Express $\frac{3a}{2} + \frac{2a}{3}$ as a single fraction

$\frac{3a}{2} + \frac{2a}{3} = \frac{9a}{6} + \frac{4a}{6} = \frac{13a}{6}$ ans. $\frac{13a}{6}$

1. Express $\frac{x}{4} + \frac{x}{3}$ as a single fraction.

2. Add:
   $\frac{2}{5a} + \frac{3}{4a}$, $a \neq 0$

3. Subtract:
   $\frac{x}{2} - \frac{x}{5}$

4. The least common denominator for the fraction $\frac{13}{8x}$ and $\frac{17}{12x}$ is:
   (1) 96x   (3) $96x^2$
   (2) 24x   (4) $24x^2$

5. Express $\frac{2a}{7} + \frac{a}{3}$ as a single fraction.

6. Express as a single fraction in lowest terms:
   $\frac{4x}{3} - \frac{x}{8}$

7. Subtract:
   $\frac{7}{6x} - \frac{6}{7x}$, $x \neq 0$

8. Add:
   $\frac{5x}{9} + \frac{4x}{3}$

9. Express as a single fraction:
   $\frac{7}{8x} - \frac{2}{5x}$, $x \neq 0$

10. Express $\frac{4a}{5} + \frac{a}{6}$ as a single fraction in simplest form.

Chapter 3
OPERATIONS IN ALGEBRA

Simplifying Radicals

REMEMBER
Make sure that one of the two factors of the radicand is the largest perfect square that you can think of:

Example: Simplify: $\sqrt{48}$
Correct: $\sqrt{48} = \sqrt{16} \cdot \sqrt{3} = 4\sqrt{3}$
Incorrect: $\sqrt{48} = \sqrt{4} \cdot \sqrt{12} = 2\sqrt{12}$

---

1. The expression $\sqrt{60}$ is equivalent to:
   (1) $4\sqrt{15}$ (3) $2\sqrt{30}$
   (2) $20\sqrt{3}$ (4) $2\sqrt{15}$

   _____

2. Simplify:
   (a) $3\sqrt{12}$ _____

   (b) $2\sqrt{125}$ _____

3. Express as a product:
   $\sqrt{54}$

   _____

4. $\sqrt{32}$ is equivalent to:
   (1) $4\sqrt{2}$ (3) $2\sqrt{16}$
   (2) $8\sqrt{4}$ (4) $16\sqrt{2}$

   _____

5. Which is a rational number?
   (1) $\sqrt{10}$ (3) $\sqrt{24}$
   (2) $\sqrt{9}$ (4) $\sqrt{120}$

   _____

6. Simplify:
   (a) $6\sqrt{40}$ _____

   (b) $2\sqrt{200}$ _____

7. Which is an irrational number?
   (1) $\sqrt{49}$ (3) $\frac{5}{16}$
   (2) 0   (4) $\sqrt{6}$

   _____

8. The expression $\sqrt{18}$ is equivalent to:
   (1) $3\sqrt{6}$ (3) $9\sqrt{2}$
   (2) $3\sqrt{2}$ (4) $2\sqrt{3}$

   _____

9. Simplify:
   (a) $8\sqrt{8}$ _____

   (b) $2\sqrt{52}$ _____

10. $\sqrt{80}$ is equivalent to:
    (1) $4\sqrt{5}$ (3) $4\sqrt{20}$
    (2) $10\sqrt{8}$ (4) $8\sqrt{10}$

    _____

Chapter 3
OPERATIONS IN ALGEBRA

Addition & Subtraction of Radicals

REMEMBER
To be able to add or subtract radicals, the radicands must be the same.

Example: add:
$$3\sqrt{2} + \sqrt{8}$$
$$3\sqrt{2} + \sqrt{4} \cdot \sqrt{2}$$
$$3\sqrt{2} + 2\sqrt{2} = 5\sqrt{2} \quad \text{ans.}$$

1. The expression $\sqrt{12} + \sqrt{27}$ is equivalent to:
   (1) $\sqrt{39}$ (3) $6\sqrt{3}$
   (2) $5\sqrt{3}$ (4) $5\sqrt{6}$

   _____

2. What is the sum of $3\sqrt{2}$ and $\sqrt{50}$?

   _____

3. Simplify:
   $$\sqrt{45} - \sqrt{20}$$

   _____

4. The sum of $5\sqrt{7}$ and $\sqrt{63}$ is:
   (1) $5\sqrt{70}$ (3) $2\sqrt{7}$
   (2) $15\sqrt{7}$ (4) $8\sqrt{7}$

   _____

5. Find the difference of $12\sqrt{11}$ and $\sqrt{44}$.
   (1) $14\sqrt{11}$ (3) $10\sqrt{11}$
   (2) $12\sqrt{33}$ (4) $12\sqrt{484}$

   _____

6. Simplify:
   (a) $6\sqrt{24} - \sqrt{96}$ _____

   (b) $2\sqrt{300} + 5\sqrt{3}$ _____

7. Find the sum of $9\sqrt{3}$ and $\sqrt{75}$

   _____

8. Simplify:
   $$\sqrt{200} - 3\sqrt{2}$$

   _____

9. The expression $\sqrt{28} + \sqrt{7}$ is equivalent to:
   (1) $\sqrt{35}$ (3) $3\sqrt{7}$
   (2) $2\sqrt{14}$ (4) $2\sqrt{49}$

   _____

10. What is the sum of $12\sqrt{5}$ and $\sqrt{125}$?
    (1) $17\sqrt{5}$ (3) $7\sqrt{5}$
    (2) $12\sqrt{130}$ (4) $12\sqrt{625}$

    _____

Chapter 3
OPERATIONS IN ALGEBRA

Mixed Operations

1. Perform the indicated operations and express as a binomial.
$$-4(x+5) - x$$

2. Simplify:
$$3x^2 - 2x + 7 - 4x^2 - 3$$

3. The expression $\sqrt{52} + \sqrt{13}$ is equivalent to:
   (1) $\sqrt{65}$ (3) $4\sqrt{13}$
   (2) $3\sqrt{13}$ (4) $2\sqrt{169}$

4. Express as a binomial.
$$3x(2x+6) - x^2 + 2x$$

5. In simplest form $5\sqrt{72}$ is:
   (1) $15\sqrt{8}$ (3) $6\sqrt{2}$
   (2) $10\sqrt{18}$ (4) $30\sqrt{2}$

6. Find the product of $(-10x^4)$ and $(-6x^2)$.

7. If $(9x+1)(4x-7)$ is written in the form $ax^2 + bx + c$, what is the value of b?
   (1) $-59x$ (3) -7
   (2) 36 (4) -59

8. Express as a monomial:
$$-3x(2x) + 4x(5x)$$

9. The expression $4\sqrt{16} - 2\sqrt{4}$ is equivalent to:
   (1) 12 (3) $2\sqrt{12}$
   (2) 20 (4) $6\sqrt{20}$

10. Express $\frac{5a}{3} + \frac{2a}{9}$ as a single fraction in simplest form.

11. Divide:
$$(45x^3 - 30x^2 + 60x) \div (-15x)$$

12. Express as a binomial:
$$3(7x-5) - (2x+1)$$

Chapter 3
OPERATIONS IN ALGEBRA

Factoring - Greatest Common Factor

REMEMBER
The greatest common factor is the largest number that divides evenly into each term. If a letter appears in all the terms, use the letter with its smallest exponent.

Example: Factor: $12x^2 + 16x^5$
$4x^2(3 + 4x^3)$ ans.

1. Factor: $7x + 14y$

2. Find the greatest common factor for 24, 36, and 48.

3. One of the factors of $5y^3 + 15y^2$ is
   (1) $15y^2$ (3) $5y^2$
   (2) $5y^3$ (4) $y^3 + 15y^2$

4. Factor: $8x - 7x^2$
   (1) $x^2(8 - 7x)$ (3) $x(8x - 7)$
   (2) $7x(1 - x)$ (4) $x(8 - 7x)$

5. Factor: $9xy + 6w^2$.

6. Find the factors of $18x^4 - 13x^3$

7. Factor: $20x^2 + 35x - 50$

8. Factor: $12x^2y + 9$
   (1) $12(x^2y + 9)$ (3) $3xy(4x + 3)$
   (2) $3(4x^2y + 3)$ (4) $9(3x^2y + 1)$

9. Factor: $14x^2 + 10x + 2$
   (1) $2(7x^2 + 5x + 1)$ (3) $2x(7x + 5 + 1)$
   (2) $2(7x^2 + 5x)$ (4) $2x(7x^2 + 5x + 1)$

10. Find the greatest common factor:
    $33abc + 44def$

35

Chapter 3
OPERATIONS IN ALGEBRA
Factoring - Difference Between Two Perfect Squares

REMEMBER
Both terms must be perfect squares and there must be a minus sign between them.

Example: Factor: $25x^2 - 4$
$(5x + 2)(5x - 2)$ ans.

1. Factor: $36x^2 - 49$

2. Factor: $x^2 - 100$

3. Factor: $4a^2 - b^2$

4. Factor: $16 - 25x^2$

5. Factor: $121m^2 - 64n^2$

6. Factor: $9x^2 - 1$

7. Factor: $y^2 - 144$

8. Factor: $81 - R^2$

9. Factor: $144y^2 - 49$

10. Factor: $x^2 - y^2$

11. Factor: $a^2b^2 - 1$

12. Factor: $4x^2 - 9$

Chapter 3
OPERATIONS IN ALGEBRA

Factoring - General Trinomials

REMEMBER
Write the trinomial in order. If the sign of the third term is positive, the signs of the factors will both be the same sign as that of the second term. If the sign of the third term is negative, the signs of the factors will be different.

Example: Factor: $x^2 - 5x + 6$ $\qquad$ $x^2 - 4x - 5$
$(x - 3)(x - 2)$ ans. $\qquad$ $(x - 5)(x + 1)$ ans.

1. Factor: $x^2 - 12x + 36$

2. Factor: $x^2 + 9x - 22$

3. Factor: $y^2 - 6y - 27$

4. Factor: $a^2 + 10a + 25$

5. Factor: (a) $3x^2 - 5x - 2$ _____
   (b) $2y^2 - 7y + 3$ _____
   (c) $3x^2 - 2x - 5$ _____

6. Factor: $y^2 - 9y + 8$

7. If one factor of $x^2 - 7x - 18$ is $x - 9$, what is the other factor?

8. Factor: $a^2 + 14a + 49$

9. Factor: (a) $2y^2 - 11y + 12$ _____
   (b) $5y^2 + 9y - 2$ _____
   (c) $7x^2 + 2x - 5$ _____

10. Factor: $x^2 + 8x - 20$

11. Factor: $c^2 - 4c - 45$

12. Factor: $x^2 + 20x + 100$

Chapter 3
OPERATIONS IN ALGEBRA

Factoring - Mixed

1. When the expressions $x^2 - 16$ and $x^2 - 7x + 12$ are factored, a common factor is:
   (1) x^2 (3) $x - 4$
   (2) $x + 4$ (4) $x - 3$

2. Factor completely:
   $$15x^3 - 10x^2 + 25x$$

3. Factor: $36a^2 - 1$

4. Factor: $x^2 - 6x - 27$

5. If one factor of $x^2 - 13x + 22$ is $(x - 11)$, what is the other factor?
   (1) $x + 2$ (3) $x - 11$
   (2) $x + 11$ (4) $x - 2$

6. Factor: $64x^2 + 36y^2$

7. Factor: $2x^2 + 7x + 3$

8. Factor: $10x^2 - 7x - 12$

9. Factor: $12x^2y^3 + 18x^3y^4$

10. Factor: $121 - 64x^2$

11. Factor: $16x^2 + 62x + 21$

12. One of the factors of $8y^3 + 24y^2$ is:
    (1) $24y^3$ (3) $24y^2$
    (2) $8y^3$ (4) $8y^2$

Chapter 3
OPERATIONS IN ALGEBRA
Chapter Test

1. Express in simplest form:
   $(7a^2 - 2a + 9) + (-3a^2 - 2) + (12a + 5)$

2. Factor: $x^2 - 5x - 36$

3. Simplify: $4\sqrt{68} + 3\sqrt{17}$

4. For which value of x is the expression $\frac{x+8}{x-3}$ undefined?
   (1) -3
   (2) -8
   (3) 3
   (4) 0

5. If $20x^9y$ is divided by $-4x^3$, the quotient is:
   (1) $-5x^3$
   (2) $-5x^6y$
   (3) $5x^3$
   (4) $5x^6y^3$

6. Factor: $25x^2 - 121$

7. If $(6y + 2)(3y + 4)$ is written in the form of $ay^2 + by + c$, what is the value of c?
   (1) 18
   (2) 30
   (3) 8y
   (4) 8

8. Express as a single fraction:
   $\frac{6x}{7} - \frac{5x}{8}$

9. Simplify: $\sqrt{600}$
   (1) 300
   (2) $6\sqrt{10}$
   (3) $10\sqrt{6}$
   (4) 30

10. Factor: $64x^2 + 16$

Chapter 3
OPERATIONS IN ALGEBRA
Chapter Test (Continued)

11. From $3x^2 - 5x + 1$, subtract $5x^2 + 3x - 7$.

12. Multiply:
$$\frac{1}{3}x (6x^3 - 9x^2 + 15x)$$

13. Which is undefined when x = 5?
    (1) x - 5   (3) $\frac{x}{3}$
    (2) $\frac{1}{x-5}$ (4) x^0

14. The least common denominator for the fractions $\frac{3}{4x}$ and $\frac{5}{6x}$ is:
    (1) $12x^2$ (3) $24x^2$
    (2) 12x   (4) 24x

15. Factor completely:
    (a) $24x^2 - 16x + 8$

    (b) $4x^2 - 49$

16. Perform the indicated operations and express as a binomial.
$$-8(2x - 3) - 4x$$

17. The expression $3\sqrt{48} - 2\sqrt{3}$ is equivalent to:
    (1) $\sqrt{45}$ (3) $14\sqrt{3}$
    (2) $\sqrt{51}$ (4) $10\sqrt{3}$

18. Divide:
$$(36x^5 - 24x^2 + 18x) \div (-6x)$$

19. If one factor of $x^2 + 10x - 39$ is (x - 3), what is the other factor?
    (1) x + 13   (3) x + 3
    (2) x - 13   (4) x - 3

20. What is the product of $\frac{3}{4}xy$ and $\frac{2}{3}x$?

Chapter 4
EQUATIONS & INEQUALITIES

Solving Equations

REMEMBER

Solve for x: 2x + 3 = 13
              -3   -3
              2x = 10
              2x/2 = 10/2
              x = 5

Solve for x: 5x + 6 = 3x + 18
              -3x   -3x
              2x + 6 = 18
                   -6   -6
              2x = 12
              2x/2 = 12/2
              x = 6

1. Find x: 7x − 9 = 12

2. Solve for x: 6x + 7 = 2x + 35

3. Solve for x: −36 = 8x − 4

4. Find the value of x: 5x + 12 = 8x − 12

5. Solve for x: 14 = 3x + 2

6. Solve for x: 8 + 2x = 16

7. Find the value of x: 4x + 8 = −2x − 4

8. Solve for x: 45 = 5 + 10x

9. Find x: −13x + 3 = 23 − 3x

10. Solve for x: 31 = 4x + 19

Chapter 4
EQUATIONS & INEQUALITIES
Solving Equations Containing Parentheses

REMEMBER
Always clear parentheses first!

Example: Solve for x:
$$3(x+2) = 18$$
$$3x + 6 = 18$$
$$ -6 \quad -6$$
$$3x = 12$$
$$\frac{3x}{3} = \frac{12}{3}$$
$$x = 4$$

1. Solve for y:
   $$4(y - 1) = 20$$

2. Solve for c:
   $$5(2 + c) = 25$$

3. Solve for x:
   $$3(x - 1) - 5 = 13$$

4. Solve for x:
   $$2(x + 4) = 3x + 18$$

5. Solve for x:
   $$7 + 6(x + 2) = 25$$

6. Solve for a:
   $$8(a - 2) = 4(a + 3)$$

7. Find the value of x:
   $$7x - 3(x + 6) = 14$$

8. Solve for x:
   $$x + 8 = 5x - 20$$

9. Solve for y:
   $$6(y + 2) + 3(2y - 3) = 39$$

10. Solve for x:
    $$80 = 10(3x + 5)$$

Chapter 4
EQUATIONS & INEQUALITIES

Solving Fractional Equations

REMEMBER
Clear all fractions by multiplying each term by the lowest common multiple.

Example: Solve for x: $\dfrac{x}{2} + \dfrac{x}{3} = 5$

The LCM = 6

$$6\left(\dfrac{x}{2}\right) + 6\left(\dfrac{x}{3}\right) = 6(5)$$

$$3x + 2x = 30$$

$$5x = 30$$

$$\dfrac{5x}{5} = \dfrac{30}{5}$$

$$x = 6$$

1. Solve for x: $\dfrac{x}{3} + \dfrac{x}{4} = 7$

2. Solve for x: $\dfrac{x}{5} - 3 = 9$

3. Solve for y: $y + \dfrac{1}{3} = \dfrac{14}{6}$

4. Solve for x: $\dfrac{2x}{3} - \dfrac{x}{5} = 7$

5. Solve for y: $\dfrac{y}{4} - \dfrac{y}{5} = 3$

6. Solve for a: $\dfrac{a}{6} + 3 = 12$

7. Solve for x: $\dfrac{3x}{2} - \dfrac{2x}{3} = 10$

8. Solve for x: $2x + \dfrac{1}{3} = \dfrac{26}{6}$

9. Solve for y: $\dfrac{y}{2} - \dfrac{y}{5} = 9$

10. Solve for x: $x + \dfrac{1}{4} = \dfrac{18}{8}$

43

Chapter 4
EQUATIONS & INEQUALITIES
Solving Fractional Equations (Continued)

REMEMBER

When a fractional equation has only one fraction equal to another fraction, solve by cross-multiplying.

Example: Solve for x:

$$\frac{x}{6} = \frac{2}{3}$$

$$3x = 12$$

$$\frac{3x}{3} = \frac{12}{3}$$

$$x = 4$$

1. Solve for x:
$$\frac{x}{12} = \frac{3}{4}$$

2. Solve for a:
$$\frac{4}{5} = \frac{a}{15}$$

3. Solve for y:
$$\frac{y+3}{6} = \frac{4}{3}$$

4. Solve for x:
$$\frac{4}{x-1} = \frac{8}{x}, x \neq 0, +1$$

5. Solve for x:
$$\frac{12}{21} = \frac{4}{x}, x \neq 0$$

6. Solve for x:
$$\frac{x}{x-2} = \frac{5}{6}, x \neq 2$$

7. Solve for y:
$$\frac{2}{3} = \frac{y}{24}$$

8. Solve for x:
$$\frac{5x+1}{8} = \frac{3}{4}$$

9. Solve for x:
$$\frac{1}{2x+4} = \frac{2}{3x}, x \neq 0, -2$$

10. Solve for x:
$$\frac{x+1}{3} = \frac{x+2}{4}$$

Chapter 4
EQUATIONS & INEQUALITIES

Solving Decimal Equations

REMEMBER
Clear all decimals first by moving the decimal points to the right the greatest number of decimal places. The decimal point on a whole number is at the right.

Example: Solve for x: $0.03x + 4 = 4.12$
The greatest number of decimal places is 2 thus

$0.03.x + 4.00. = 4.12.$
$3x + 400 = 412$
$ -400 -400$
$3x = 12$
$\frac{3x}{3} = \frac{12}{3}$
$x = 4$

1. Solve for x:
   $0.4x + 8 = 16$

2. Solve for a:
   $3a + 0.2 = 2.3$

3. Solve for x:
   $0.06x = 49.2$

4. Solve for x:
   $0.03x = 24$

5. Solve for y:
   $0.25y - 2 = 4$

6. Solve for x:
   $x - 0.2 = 2.8$

7. Solve for y:
   $0.5y - 2.5 = 3.5$

8. Solve for y:
   $0.07y + 2.1 = 7$

9. Solve for x:
   $2.5x = 50$

10. Solve for x:
    $0.09x + 3 = 4.8$

Chapter 4
EQUATIONS & INEQUALITIES

Solving Literal Equations

REMEMBER

Literal equations are solved like all other equations -- all letters are to be treated as numbers except the letter to be solved.

Example: Solve for a in terms of b and c:

$$4a + 5b = c$$
$$ -5b -5b$$
$$4a = c - 5b$$
$$\frac{4a}{4} = \frac{c-5b}{4}$$
$$a = \frac{c-5b}{4}$$

1. Solve for a in terms of b and c:
   $3a - 2b = 4c$

2. Solve for K in terms of M, N, and P:
   $M = NKP$

3. Solve for x in terms of a, b, and c:
   $bx + c = a$

4. Solve for b in terms of A and h:
   $A = \frac{bh}{2}$

5. If $ay - bx = 3$, then y is equal to:
   (1) $\frac{3}{a} + bx$ (3) $\frac{3+bx}{a}$
   (2) $\frac{3}{a} - bx$ (4) $\frac{3-bx}{a}$

6. Solve for E in terms of M and P:
   $\frac{E}{P} = M$

7. Solve for x in terms of a, b, and c:
   $ax - b = c$

8. Solve for h in terms of v, l, and w:
   $v = lwh$

9. Solve for y in terms of a and b:
   $3a + 4y = 2b$

10. Solve for x in terms of a, b, and c:
    $abx - c = 5$

Chapter 4
EQUATIONS & INEQUALITIES

Solving Inequalities

> **REMEMBER**
> Inequalities are solved like all other equations. Change the order of the inequality when you multiply or divide by a negative number.
>
> **Example:** Solve for x:
>
> $3x + 5 > 17$
> $\quad\;\; -5 \;\; -5$
> $3x > 12$
> $\dfrac{3x}{3} > \dfrac{12}{3}$
> $x > 4$
>
> $9 - 4x < 17$
> $-9 \quad\;\; -9$
> $-4x < 8$
> $\dfrac{-4x}{-4} < \dfrac{8}{-4}$
> $x > -2$

---

1. Solve for x:

    $4x + 6 < 30$

2. Solve for y:

    $4y - 3 \leq y + 18$

3. The largest possible value of x in the solution set of $3x + 1 \leq 10$:

    (1) 1 (3) 3
    (2) 2 (4) 4

4. Which inequality is equivalent to $2x - 1 > 7$?

    (1) x < 4 (3) x < 3
    (2) x > 3 (4) x > 4

5. If y is an integer, what is the solution set of $-2 \leq y < 1$?

    (1) -1,0,1 (3) -1,0
    (2) -2,-1,0,1 (4) -2,-1,0

6. Solve for x:

    $7x - 8 \leq 9x - 4$

7. Which inequality is equivalent to $8x + 24 > 8$?

    (1) x > -2 (3) x > -4
    (2) x < -2 (4) x < -4

8. A member of the solution set of $3 < x \leq 6$ is:

    (1) 1 (3) 3
    (2) 2 (4) 6

9. Solve for x:

    $10x - 7 > 3x + 35$

    (1) x < 6 (3) x < 4
    (2) x > 4 (4) x > 6

10. Which is equivalent to $3x - 12 < 3$?

    (1) x < 5 (3) x < -5
    (2) x > 5 (4) x > -5

Chapter 4
EQUATIONS & INEQUALITIES

One Variable Inequalities

REMEMBER

To read a one variable inequality, note the value or values at the end points and use the notation below: The open circle at the end of the line graph means leave out the equal sign under the inequality symbol.

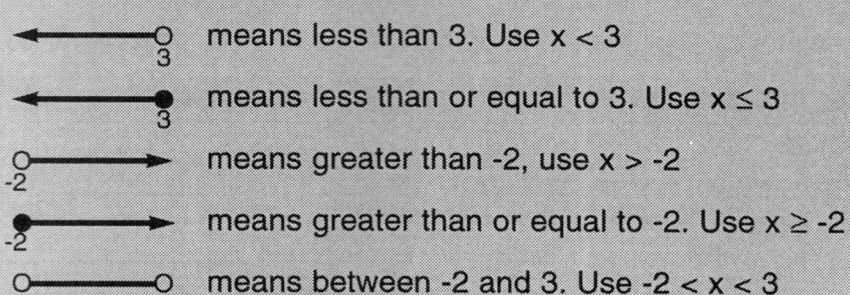

- means less than 3. Use $x < 3$
- means less than or equal to 3. Use $x \leq 3$
- means greater than -2, use $x > -2$
- means greater than or equal to -2. Use $x \geq -2$
- means between -2 and 3. Use $-2 < x < 3$
- means between -2 and 3 and including -2 and 3. Use $-2 \leq x \leq 3$ 

---

1. Which variable inequality is represented below?

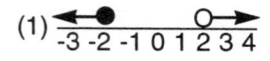

   (1) $-2 > x \geq 1$ (3) $-2 < x \leq 1$
   (2) $-2 \geq x > 1$ (4) $-2 \leq x < 1$

2. Which graph is represented by the open sentence $-1 \leq x < 4$?

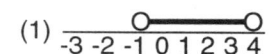

3. Which graph is represented by the open sentence $-2 \leq x \leq 2$?

4. Which open sentence is represented by the graph below?

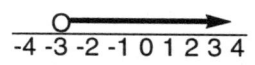

   (1) $x \geq -3$ (3) $x \leq -3$
   (2) $x > -3$ (4) $x < -3$

48

Chapter 4
EQUATIONS & INEQUALITIES

One Variable Inequalities (Continued)

5. Which open sentence is represented by the graph below?

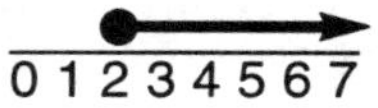

   (1) x > 2   (3) x ≤ 2
   (2) x < 2   (4) x ≥ 2

6. Which open sentence is represented by the graph below?

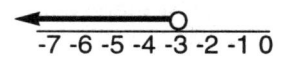

   (1) x > -3   (3) x < -3
   (2) x ≥ -3   (4) x ≤ -3

7. Which graph represents the disjunction (x ≤ -2) ∨ (x ≥ 3)?

   (1) 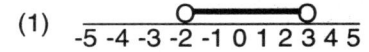
   (2) 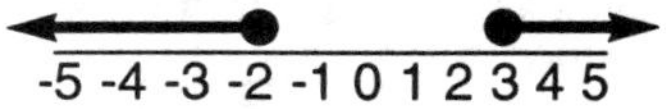
   (3) 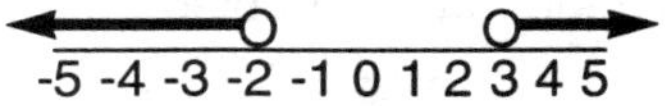
   (4)

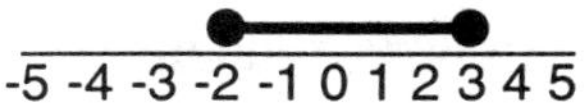

8. Which graph is represented by the open sentence -5 ≤ x < 0?

   (1) 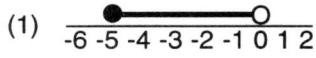
   (2) 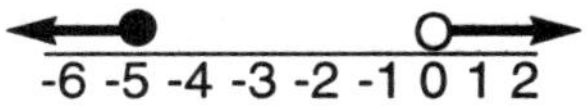
   (3) 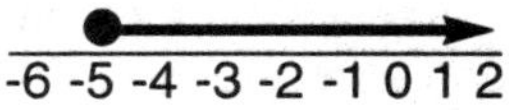
   (4)

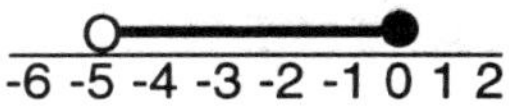

9. Which one variable inequality is represented below?

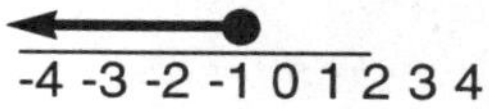

   (1) x < -1   (3) x ≤ -1
   (2) x > -1   (4) x ≥ -1

10. Which graph represents the disjunction (x < -3) ∨ (x ≥ 4)?

    (1)   (3)
    (2)   (4)

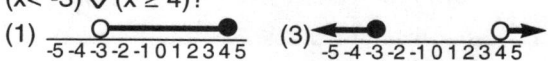

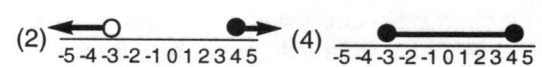

11. Which open sentence is represented by the graph below?

    (1) -4 ≤ x ≤ 2   (3) -4 > x > 2
    (2) -4 < x < 2   (4) -4 ≥ x ≥ 2

12. Which one variable inequality is represented below?

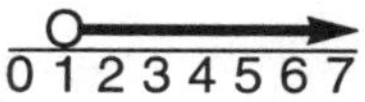

    (1) x < 1   (3) x ≥ 1
    (2) x ≤ 1   (4) x > 1

13. Which one variable inequality is represented below?

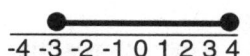

    (1) -3 < x < 4   (3) -3 < x ≤ 4
    (2) -3 ≤ x < 4   (4) -3 ≤ x ≤ 4

Chapter 4
EQUATIONS & INEQUALITIES

Direct Variation

> **REMEMBER**
>
> Two quantities vary directly with one another if the ratio of any two corresponding values of these variables is constant, that is
>
> $$\frac{y_1}{x_1} = \frac{y_2}{x_2} \text{ or } \frac{y_1}{y_2} = \frac{x_1}{x_2}$$
>
> **Example:** Find the perimeter of a square if the length of its side is 5 and a second square has a perimeter of 25 and a side of 10.
>
> $$\frac{\text{perimeter 1}}{\text{perimeter 2}} = \frac{\text{side 1}}{\text{side 2}}$$
>
> $\frac{p}{25} = \frac{5}{10}$ $\quad 10p = 5(25)$
> $\quad\quad\quad\quad 10p = 125$
> $\quad\quad\quad\quad\quad p = 12.5$ <u>ans.</u>

---

1. A car travels 200 miles in 5 hours. If the car travels at a constant speed, how far will it travel in 3 hours?

2. If 7 men can build a house in 42 days, how many days would it take the 7 men to build 9 houses?
   - (1) 6
   - (2) 63
   - (3) 294
   - (4) 378

3. A house worth $50,000 has a school tax of $700 per year. What is the school tax per year for a house worth $75,000?

4. If fertilizer for 2,500 square feet of lawn costs $5.25, what is the cost of fertilizer for 6,000 square feet of lawn?
   - (1) $10.50
   - (2) $12.60
   - (3) $15.75
   - (4) $25.81

5. The scale on a map shows that 1" represents 16 miles. How far apart are two towns if they are 6.5 inches apart on the map?

6. A backhoe excavates 800 cubic yards of earth in 6 hours. How many cubic yards can be excavated in $7\frac{1}{2}$ hours?

7. A machine can manufacture 1200 washers in 20 minutes. How many minutes will it take to manufacturer 2700 washers?

8. If interest on a loan varies directly as the rate, what change takes place in the interest when the rate is doubled?
   - (1) halved
   - (2) doubled
   - (3) remains same
   - (4) multiplied by four

9. y varies directly as x. If y = -25 when x = 3, find y when x = -12.

10. If 4 men earn a total of $975 in a week, what will 32 men, working at the same rate of pay, earn in a week?

Chapter 4
EQUATIONS & INEQUALITIES

Number and Consecutive Integer Problems

> **REMEMBER**
> If x represents and even integer, then x + 2 represents the next consecutive even integer. If x represents an odd integer, then x + 2 represents the next consecutive odd integer. If x represents an integer, then x + 1 represents the next consecutive integer.

1. If x represents an even integer, which expression represents an odd integer?
   (1) x^2 (3) x + 1
   (2) x - 2   (4) 2x

2. If x represents a number, which expression represents a number which is 7 less than 2 times x?
   (1) 2x - 7   (3) 2 - 7x
   (2) 7 - 2x   (4) 7x - 2

3. If 3n represents an odd integer, which represents the next larger consecutive odd integer?
   (1) 3n - 1   (3) 3n + 2
   (2) 4n   (4) 3n + 1

4. If a certain number is decreased by 13, the result is 17. What is the number?

5. Find the value in cents of d dimes and q quarters.

6. If 6 is added to 2 times a certain number, the result is 14. Find the number.

7. If x represents an even number, which expression represents an even number?
   (1) 3x + 2   (3) x - 3
   (2) 3x + 1   (4) x + 5

8. If n represents a number, which expression represents a number which is 6 more than 5 times n?
   (1) 6n + 5   (3) 5 - 6n
   (2) 5n - 6   (4) 5n + 6

9. If 9 less than 3 times a certain number is 15, find the number.
   (1) -2   (3) 8
   (2) 2   (4) -8

10. How much money would you have if you had n nickels and h half-dollars?

Chapter 4
EQUATIONS & INEQUALITIES

Solving Simple Systems of Equations

REMEMBER

To solve a simple system of equations, add or subtract the equations and eliminate one of the two variable.

Example: Solve for x:
$5x + y = 9$
$3x - y = 7$

$5x + \cancel{y} = 9$
$3x - \cancel{y} = 7$
$8x = 16$
$\dfrac{8x}{8} = \dfrac{16}{8}$
$x = 2$

1. Solve for x:

    $3x - 2y = 7$
    $x + 2y = 5$

2. Solve for x:

    $6x + y = 5$
    $3x + y = 2$

3. Solve for y:

    $2x + 4y = 6$
    $-2x + y = 4$

4. Solve for y:

    $7x + 2y = 1$
    $7x - y = -11$

5. Solve for a:

    $2a + 3b = 6$
    $4a - 3b = 12$

6. Solve for b:

    $a + 4b = 7$
    $a - 3b = -21$

7. Solve for x:

    $8x + y = 19$
    $3x - y = 3$

8. Solve for b:

    $5b + a = 19$
    $2b + a = 1$

9. Solve for x:

    $7x - y = 17$
    $2x + y = 10$

10. Solve for y:

    $9x + 5y = 12$
    $9x + 3y = -6$

Chapter 4
EQUATIONS & INEQUALITIES

Mixed Problems

1. Solve for y:
$$\frac{y}{5} + \frac{y}{3} = 8$$

2. Solve for x:
$$-8x + 27 = -10x + 9$$

3. Which is equivalent to 6x + 12 > -24?
   (1) x < -6   (3) x > -2
   (2) x > -6   (4) x < -2

4. Solve for a:
$$0.03a + 9 = 1.5$$

5. Solve for x:
$$9(x - 1) + 5(2x + 6) = 59$$

6. Solve for x:
$$\frac{3}{x-2} = \frac{5}{x+5}, \; x \neq 2, -5$$

7. If ax + 2by = 8, then y is equal to:
   (1) $\frac{8+ax}{2b}$ (3) $\frac{8}{b} - ax$
   (2) $\frac{4-ax}{b}$ (4) $\frac{8-ax}{2b}$

8. If x varies directly as y and x = 21 when y is 7, find x when y is 5.

9. If an even integer is represented by 7x - 2, what is the next largest even integer represented by?
   (1) 7x - 4   (3) 9x
   (2) 8x - 2   (4) 7x

10. Solve for x:
$$11x - 5y = 18$$
$$-6x - 5y = -16$$

11. Which one variable inequality is represented below?

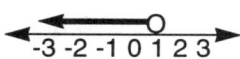

    ←——o———→
    -3 -2 -1 0 1 2 3

   (1) x < 1   (3) x > 1
   (2) x ≤ 1   (4) x ≥ 1

53

Chapter 4
EQUATIONS & INEQUALITIES

Chapter Test

1. Solve for x:
   $$6x - 3 = x + 12$$

2. Which open sentence is represented by the graph below?

   (number line from -4 to 4, open circle at -3, closed circle at 1)

   (1) $-3 \leq x \leq 1$ (3) $-3 < x \leq 1$
   (2) $-3 < x < 1$ (4) $-3 \leq x < 1$

3. Solve the following systems of equations for x:
   $$4x + y = 7$$
   $$2x - y = 5$$

4. Solve for y:
   $$0.3y + 4 = 19$$

5. Solve for x:
   $$8(x - 3) - 7 = 9$$

6. Solve for R in terms of C and D:
   $$3C = 2DR$$

7. Solve for y:
   $$\frac{y}{15} = \frac{4}{15}$$

8. Solve for x:
   $$-4x + 8 > 16$$

   (1) $x > 2$ (3) $x > -2$
   (2) $x < -2$ (4) $x < 2$

9. If 3 men can build 2 barns in one week, how many men working at the same rate will be needed to build 8 barns in one week?

10. Solve for x:
    $$8(x + 5) - 2(x - 10) = 96$$

11. If $2x + 1$ represents an odd integer, which of the following represents the next consecutive odd integer?

    (1) $2x - 1$ (3) $3x$
    (2) $2x + 3$ (4) $3x - 1$

54

Chapter 4
EQUATIONS & INEQUALITIES
Chapter Test (Continued)

12. Solve the following systems of equations for x:

    $x + 8y = 17$

    $3x - 8y = 15$

13. If x varies directly as y and x = 3 when y = 18, find y when x = -2.

14. On the graph below, represent the inequality $-2 < x \leq 2$.

    -3 -2 -1 0 1 2 3

15. Solve for x:

    $0.2x = 0.01x + 38$

16. Which inequality is equivalent to $\frac{3x}{4} - 3 < 6$?

    (1) x < 4   (3) x < 8
    (2) x < 7   (4) x < 12

17. Solve for y:

    $3(5 - y) = 7(y - 5)$

18. Solve for n:

    $\frac{8n}{3n+6} = \frac{10}{3}$

19. If 8 is subtracted from 3 times a certain number, the result is 25. Find the number.

20. Given the equation $3a + b = c$, solve for a in terms of b and c.

21. If 6x - 1 represents an odd integer, represent the next integer.

22. Solve for x:

    $-11x + 18 = -2x - 27$

55

Chapter 5
ANGLES & TRIANGLES

Complementary and Supplementary Angles

REMEMBER

Two angles are called complementary angles if the sum of their measures is 90°.

Two angles are called supplementary angles if the sum of their measures is 180°.

Example: The measures of two complementary angles are in the ratio of 1:5. Find the measure in degrees of the smaller angle.

Let x = smaller angle   x + 5x = 90
    5x = larger angle   6x = 90
                                     x = 15
                         smaller angle = 15°

---

1. The measure of two complementary angles are in the ratio 1:8. Find the measure of the larger angle.

   _____

2. The measure of two supplementary angles are in the ration of 1:4. Find the number of degrees in the smaller angle.

   _____

3. Two angles are complementary and congruent. How many degrees are there in each angle?

   _____

4. What is the supplement of an angle that measures 7x?

   (1) 7x - 90   (3) 7x - 180
   (2) 90 - 7x   (4) 180 - 7x

   _____

5. In the accompanying diagram, $\overleftrightarrow{AOB}$ is a straight line, m∠AOD = 5x - 24 and m∠BOD = x. What is the value of x?

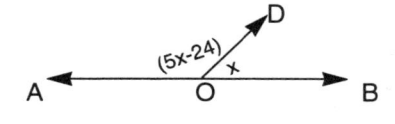

   _____

6. In the accompanying diagram, $\overleftrightarrow{ABC}$ is a straight line, $\overrightarrow{BD} \perp \overrightarrow{BE}$, and m∠CBE = 35. Find m∠ABD.

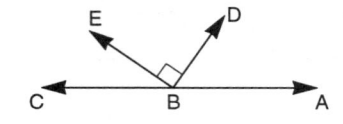

   _____

7. Two complementary angles are in the ratio 5:4. The number of degrees in the *larger* angle is:

   (1) 10   (3) 50
   (2) 20   (4) 40

   _____

8. Two angles are supplementary. If one of these angles measures 70 more than the other, find the measure of the *smaller* angle.

   _____

9. Two angles are complementary. If one of these angles measures 30 more than the other, find the measure of the *larger* angle.

   _____

10. Two angles are supplementary and the measure of one angle is four times the measure of the other. Find the measure of the *smaller* angle.

    _____

Chapter 5
ANGLES & TRIANGLES

Vertical Angles

REMEMBER

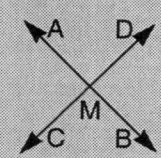

In the diagram above, lines $\overleftrightarrow{AB}$ and $\overleftrightarrow{CD}$ intersect at M. ∠AMC and ∠DMB are opposite each other and are called vertical angles. ∠AMC and ∠DMB are also equal in measure.

Example: In the diagram above, vertical angles AMD and CMB are represented by $(2x + 20)$ and $(x + 60)$ respectively. Find the value of x.

$$2x + 20 = x + 60$$
$$2x - x = 60 - 20$$
$$x = 40 \text{ Ans.}$$

1. As shown in the diagram $\overleftrightarrow{XY}$ and $\overleftrightarrow{WZ}$ intersect at E. If ∠XEW is represented by $(2x + 40)$ and ∠ZEY by $(6x - 20)$, find the value of x.

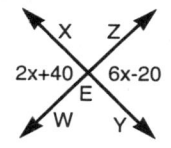

2. Two vertical angles are represented by $(3x - 10)$ and $(x + 30)$. Find the value of x.

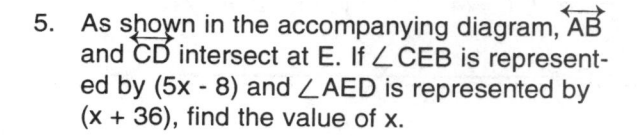

3. In the diagram, ∠1 = $(5x + 5)$ and ∠2 = $(2x + 35)$. Find the number of degrees in ∠1.

4. In the accompanying diagram, $\overleftrightarrow{QR}$ intersects $\overleftrightarrow{ST}$ at V, and m∠QVS = 30. If m∠TVR = $5x - 40$, find x.

5. As shown in the accompanying diagram, $\overleftrightarrow{AB}$ and $\overleftrightarrow{CD}$ intersect at E. If ∠CEB is represented by $(5x - 8)$ and ∠AED is represented by $(x + 36)$, find the value of x.

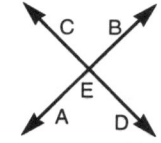

6. In the accompanying diagram, $\overleftrightarrow{AB}$ intersects $\overleftrightarrow{CD}$ at E. If m∠AEC = 100 and m∠DEB = 5x, what is the value of x?

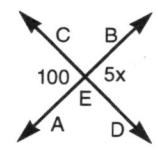

Chapter 5
ANGLES & TRIANGLES

Alternate Interior Angles

REMEMBER
Alternate interior angles formed by a transversal and parallel lines are equal. When traced, they look like a Z or ⌠.

Example:

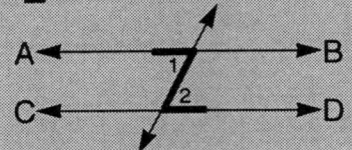

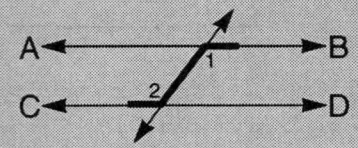

If line AB ∥ CD, then in both cases above ∠1 & ∠2 are alternate interior angles and are equal.

---

1. In the diagram below, m∠CFE = 5x and m∠BEF = x + 20. If AB ∥ CD, find the value of x.

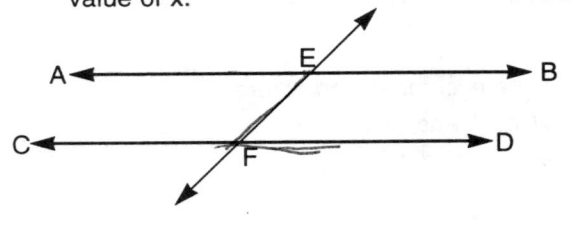

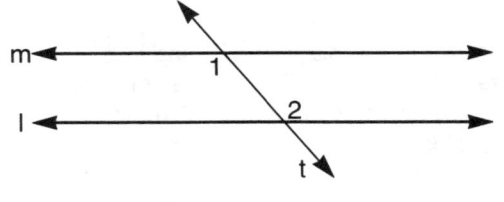

2. As shown in the accompanying diagram, CD ∥ EF and intersected by transversal GH. If m∠1 = (4x+30) and m∠2 = (2x+50), find x.

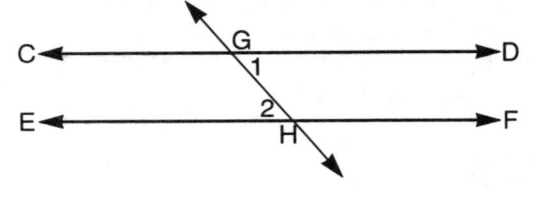

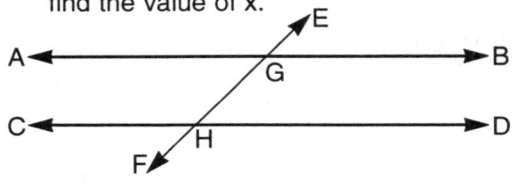

3. In the accompany diagram, AB ∥ CD, HG intersects AB at E and CD at F. If m∠CFE = 105 and m∠BEF = (2x + 5), find x.

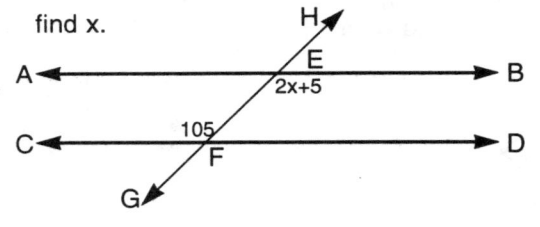

4. In the accompanying diagram, parallel lines m and l are cut by transversal t. If m∠1 = (3x - 20) and the m∠2 = (x + 100), find the degree measure of ∠2.

5. In the accompanying diagram, AB ∥ CD and EF intersects AB at G and CD at H. If m∠AGH is (4x - 10) and m∠GHD is 70, find the value of x.

6. In the accompanying diagram, AB is parallel to CD, m∠BAC = 51, and m∠BCD = 70. Find the measure of ∠ACB.

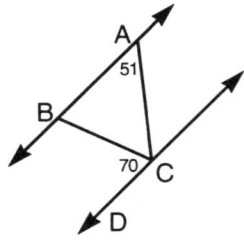

Chapter 5
ANGLES & TRIANGLES

Corresponding Angles

REMEMBER
Corresponding angles formed by a transversal and parallel lines are equal. When traced, they look like an F, forward, backward or upside down.

Examples:

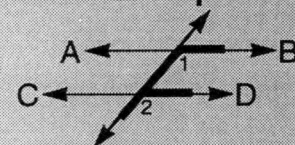

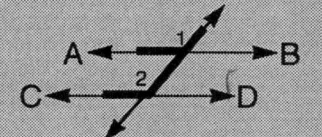

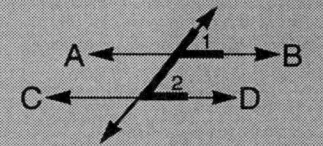

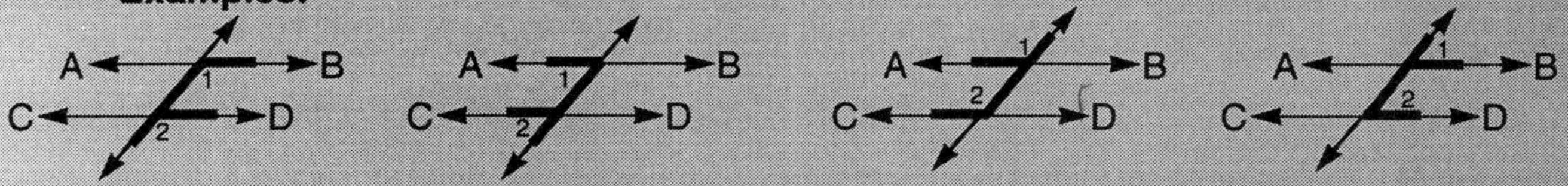

If line AB ∥ CD, then in all cases above ∠1 and ∠2 are corresponding angles and are equal.

1. In the accompanying diagram $\overleftrightarrow{AB} \parallel \overleftrightarrow{CD}$ and are intersected by GH at points E and F respectively. If m∠AEG = (3x+5) and m∠CFE = 95, find x.

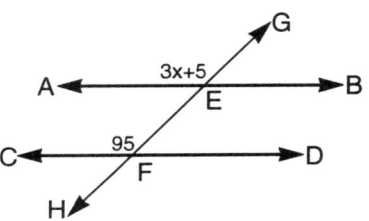

2. In the accompanying diagram, $\overleftrightarrow{CD} \parallel \overleftrightarrow{EF}$ and is intersected by transversal $\overleftrightarrow{GH}$. If m∠1 = (2x+20) and m∠2 = (x+40), what is the degree measure of ∠2?

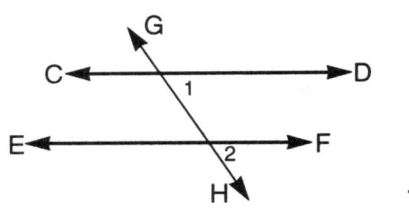

3. In the diagram below, $\overleftrightarrow{AB} \parallel \overleftrightarrow{CD}$. If m∠1 = (6x-30) and m∠2 = (3x+15) find the number of degrees in m∠1.

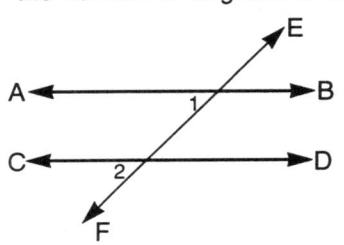

4. In the accompanying diagram, transversal $\overleftrightarrow{RS}$ intersects parallel lines $\overleftrightarrow{XY}$ and $\overleftrightarrow{WZ}$ at E and H, respectively. If m∠HEY = 81, what is the m∠ZHS?

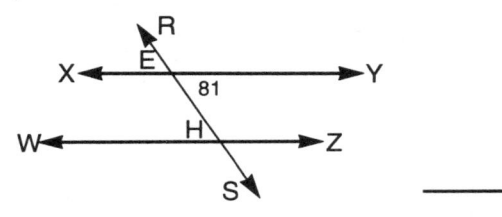

5. In the diagram below, m∠EGB = (3x+20) and m∠GHD = (2x+40). If $\overleftrightarrow{AB} \parallel \overleftrightarrow{CD}$, find the value of x.

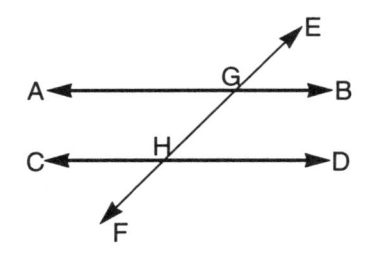

6. In the accompanying diagram, $\overleftrightarrow{XY} \parallel \overleftrightarrow{WZ}$ and meet transversal $\overleftrightarrow{AB}$ in points R and P respectively. If m∠YRP = 120 and m∠ZPB = 4x-20, find the value of x.

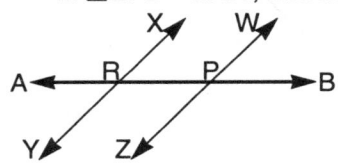

Chapter 5
ANGLES & TRIANGLES
Interior Angles on the Same Side of the Transversal

REMEMBER
Interior angles on the same side of the transversal formed by the transversal and parallel lines are supplementary. When traced, they look like a ⊏ or a ⊐.

Examples:

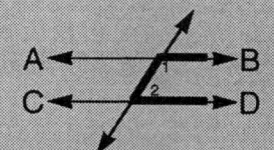

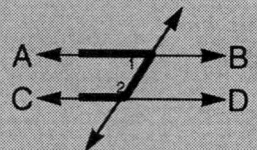

If line $\overleftrightarrow{AB} \parallel \overleftrightarrow{CD}$, then in both cases above ∠1 and ∠2 are interior angles on the same side of the transversal and add up to 180°.

---

1. In the accompanying diagram, line l is parallel to line m and they are intersected by transversal t. If m∠1 = 42, find the measure of ∠2.

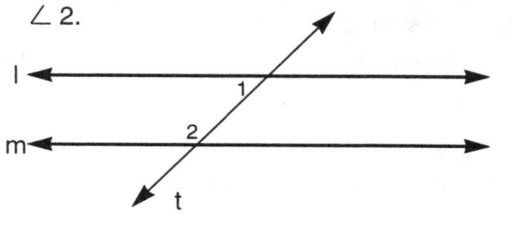

2. In the diagram below, the m∠1 = (3x+20) and m∠2 = (2x+30). If AB ∥ CD, find the value of x.

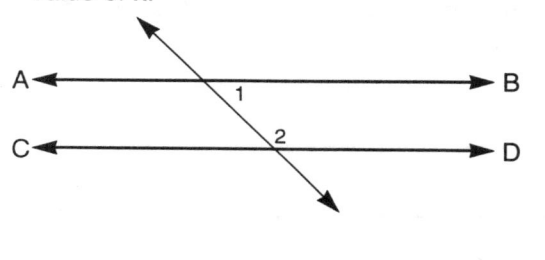

3. In the accompanying diagram, line a is parallel to line b and they are intersected by transversal c. If m∠1 = (4x-10) and m∠2 = 110, find the value of x.

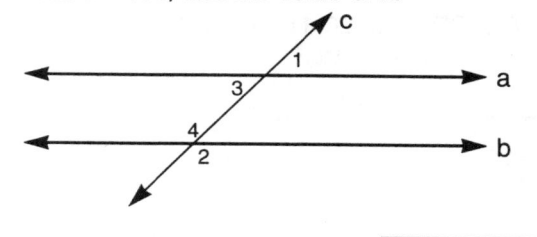

4. In the accompanying diagram, $\overleftrightarrow{AD} \parallel \overleftrightarrow{CD}$ and intersects transversal $\overleftrightarrow{GH}$ at points E and F, respectively. If m∠AEF = 124 and m∠EFC = (2x+20), find the value of x.

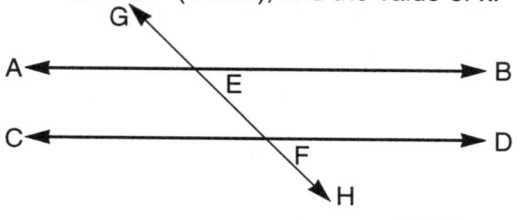

5. In the accompanying diagram, $\overleftrightarrow{AB} \parallel \overleftrightarrow{CD}$ and transversal $\overleftrightarrow{EF}$ intersects $\overleftrightarrow{AB}$ at G and $\overleftrightarrow{CD}$ at H. If m∠1 = (4x+50) and m∠2 = (x+30), find the value of x.

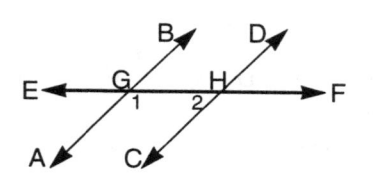

6. In the accompanying diagram, $\overleftrightarrow{AB} \parallel \overleftrightarrow{CD}$ and intersects transversal $\overleftrightarrow{GH}$ at points E and F respectively. Name two pairs of interior angles on the same side of the transversal.

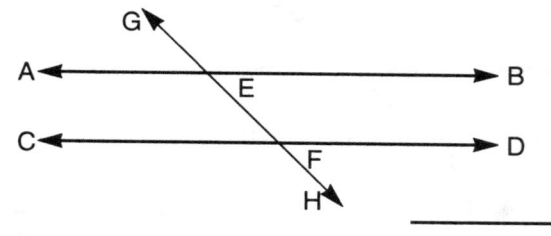

Chapter 5
ANGLES & TRIANGLES

Angles and the Triangle

REMEMBER

Every triangle has three angles and the sum of the measures of the angles of a triangle is 180°.

Example: The measures of the angles of a triangle are represented by x, 3x and (x + 60). find the number of degrees in the measures of the smallest angle of the triangle.

$$x + 3x + x + 60 = 180$$
$$5x + 60 = 180$$
$$5x = 120$$
$$x = 24 \text{ ans.}$$

1. The degree measures of the angles of a triangle are represented by x, 2x and 3x. Find the number of degrees in the smallest angle.

2. In triangle ABC, m∠A = x, m∠B = (x+10) and m∠C = (3x+20). What is the number of degrees in the measure of ∠A?

3. If two angles of a triangle are complimentary, what is the degree measure of the third angle?

4. Two angles of a triangle are equal in measure and the third angle is 110. Find the number of degrees in one of the two equal angles.

5. If the angles of a triangle are in the ratio 2:3:5, how many degrees are there in the largest angle of the triangle?

6. In triangle EDF, m∠E = (x+10), m∠D = (3x+30) and m∠F = (5x+50). How many degrees are there in ∠F?

7. Could two angles of a triangle ever be supplementary? (yes or no)

8. The three angles of a triangle are in the ratio of 5:6:7. Find the number of degrees in the smallest angle of the triangle.

9. If the angles of a triangle are represented by x, 6x+15 and 8x, the triangle must be:
   (1) acute   (3) obtuse
   (2) isosceles (4) right

10. If two angles of a triangle are complementary, then the triangle *must* be:
    (1) equilateral (3) isosceles
    (2) right   (4) obtuse

11. In the accompanying diagram, $\overline{CD}$ is the bisector of ∠ACB, m∠A = 62 and m∠B = 84. Find m∠ACD.

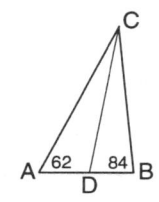

Chapter 5
ANGLES & TRIANGLES

Special Kinds of Triangles

REMEMBER

(1) An **isosceles** triangle is a triangle that has two equal sides and the angles opposite the equal sides are also equal. The angle between the equal sides is called the vertex angle.

(2) An **equilateral** triangle is a triangle that has three equal sides and three equal angles.

(3) A **right** triangle is a triangle that contains a right angle.

Example: The vertex angle of an isosceles triangle is 80. How many degrees are in each of the base angles?

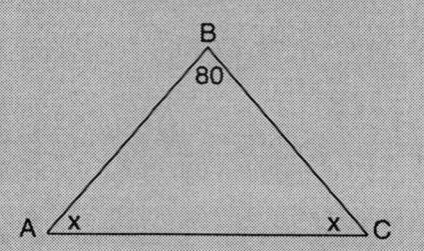

Isosceles $\triangle ABC$ with $\overline{AB} = \overline{BC}$. $\angle B$ is the vertex angle and is equal to 80. $\angle A$ and $\angle C$, the base angles are equal.

Therefore:
$$x + x + 80 = 180.$$
$$2x = 100$$
$$x = 50 \text{ in each base}$$

---

1. The measure of the vertex angle of an isosceles triangle is 50. Find the measure in degrees of one of the base angles of the triangle.

2. The measure of each base angle of an isosceles triangle is 20. Find the number of degrees in the measure of the vertex angle.

3. In the accompanying diagram, triangle GHI is isosceles with side $\overline{HI}$ as the base. If m$\angle$H = 30, find m$\angle$G.

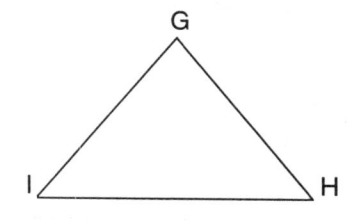

4. If the measure of each base angle of an isosceles triangle is represented by x, then the measure of the vertex angle is represented by:

   (1) 2x - 180   (3) 180 - x
   (2) 2x   (4) 180 - 2x

5. Two angles of a right triangle are congruent. What is the number of degrees in the measure of each of these angles?

6. In the accompanying diagram, angle BCD is an exterior angle of triangle ABC and is therefore supplementary to angle BCA. If m$\angle$A = 25 and m$\angle$B = 85, find the number of degrees in the measure of angle BCD.

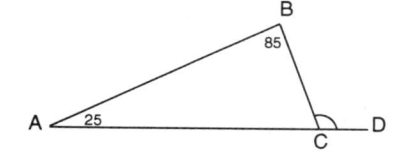

Chapter 5
ANGLES & TRIANGLES
Special Kinds of Triangles (Continued)

7. In an equilateral triangle, what is the degree measure of any one of its exterior angles?

   _____

8. In the accompanying diagram, side $\overline{AC}$ of triangle ABC is extended to D and the measure of angle BCD is 125. What is the measure in degrees of angle BCA?

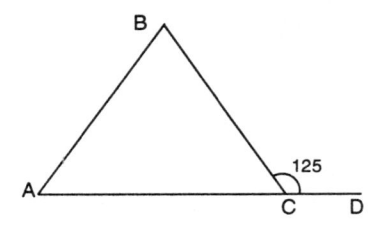

   _____

9. In the diagram below of △CDE, m∠C = 70 and m∠D = 30. Find the measure of exterior angle DEF.

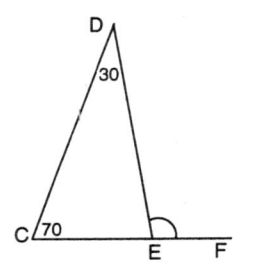

   _____

10. In the accompanying diagram, $\overrightarrow{DH}$ ∥ $\overline{EF}$. If m∠HDF = 30 and m∠EDF = 53, find m∠E.

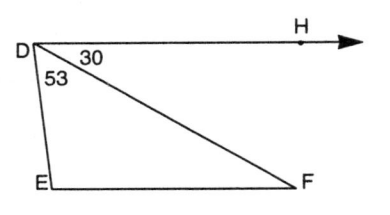

    _____

11. △ABC is a right △ with a right angle at C. If exterior angle ABD = 130, how many degrees are there in ∠A?

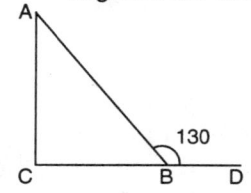

    _____

12. What is the number of degrees in the acute angle of an isosceles right triangle?

    _____

13. In the accompanying diagram of isosceles triangle ABC, $\overline{AB}$ ≅ $\overline{CB}$, point D is on $\overrightarrow{AB}$, and m∠CBD = 124. Find m∠A.

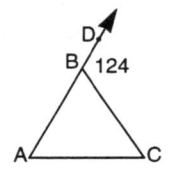

    _____

14. The measure of the vertex angle of an isosceles triangle is 70. Find the measure of a base angle of the triangle.

    _____

15. In the accompanying diagram of △ABC, the measure of exterior angle BCD is 100 and m∠BAC = 35. Find m∠ABC.

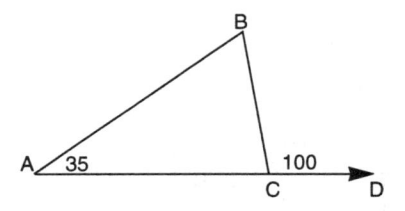

    _____

63

Chapter 5
ANGLES & TRIANGLES

Pythagorean Theorem

REMEMBER

In a right triangle the sum of the squares of the two legs is equal to the square of the hypotenuse.

$$a^2 + b^2 = c^2$$

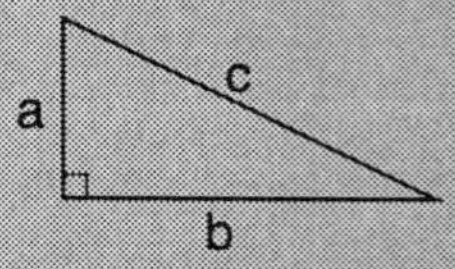

Example: The lengths of two legs of a right triangle are 2 and 7. Find in radical form, the length of the hypotenuse.

$a^2 + b^2 = c^2$
$2^2 + 7^2 = c^2$
$4 + 49 = c^2$
$53 = c^2$
$c = \sqrt{53}$

---

1. A wire reaches from the top of a 26 meter telephone pole to a point on the ground 8 meters from the base of the pole. What is the length of the wire to the nearest tenth of a meter?

2. The lengths of the legs of a right triangle are 3 and 6. Find, in radical form, the length of the hypotenuse of the right triangle.

3. In the accompanying diagram of rectangle ABCD, AB = 6 and BC = 8. What is the length of $\overline{AC}$?

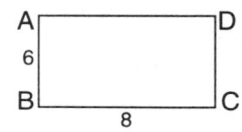

4. Express in radical form, the length of one leg of a right triangle if the hypotenuse is 9 and the other leg is 5.

5. Find the length, in radical form, of the hypotenuse of an isosceles right triangle whose leg equals 3.

6. The dimensions of a rectangle are 14 centimeters by 48 centimeters. Find, in centimeters, the length of the diagonal of the rectangle.

7. In the accompanying diagram, △ABC is a right triangle with the right angle at C. If AB = 13, BC = 12, find AC.

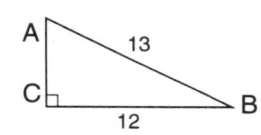

8. The hypotenuse of a right triangle is 25. If one leg is 20, the other leg is:
   (1) $\sqrt{5}$ (3) 15
   (2) $\sqrt{1025}$ (4) 45

9. The length of the hypotenuse of a right triangle is 7 and the length of one leg is 4. What is the length of the other leg?
   (1) 11   (3) 3
   (2) $\sqrt{65}$ (4) $\sqrt{33}$

10. Which of the following could be the lengths of the sides of a right triangle?
    (1) 3, 5, 8   (3) 2, 4, 6
    (2) 5, 12, 13   (4) 5, 5, 5

Chapter 5
ANGLES & TRIANGLES

Similarity

> **REMEMBER**
> If two polygons are similar, then their corresponding angles are equal and their corresponding sides are in proportion.
>
> **Example:** In the accompanying diagram $\triangle$RST is similar to $\triangle$DEF. If DE = 10, DF = 2, RS = 5, $\angle R \cong \angle D$ and $\angle S \cong \angle E$, find RT.
>
> $\frac{x}{2} = \frac{5}{10}$
> $10x = 10$
> $x = 1$ Ans.

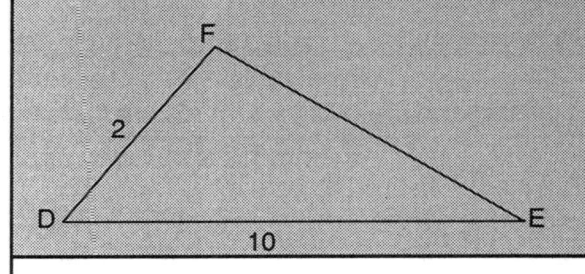

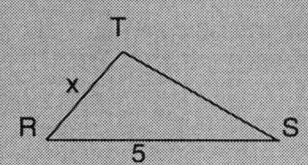

1. A photograph 5 inches wide and 7 inches long is to be enlarges so that the length is 14 inches. The new width will be:
   (1) 10 in   (3) 14 in
   (2) 12 in   (4) 21 in

2. If the ratio of the areas of two similar triangles is 9:64, the ratio of two corresponding sides could be:
   (1) 9:64   (3) 81:4096
   (2) 18:128 (4) 3:8

3. In the accompanying diagram, $\triangle$ABC is similar to $\triangle$DEF. If AC = 9, AB = 5, CB = 7, DE =15, $\angle B \cong \angle E$, and $\angle A \cong \angle D$, find FE.

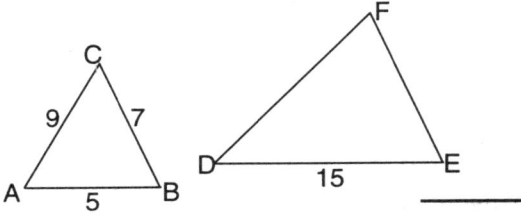

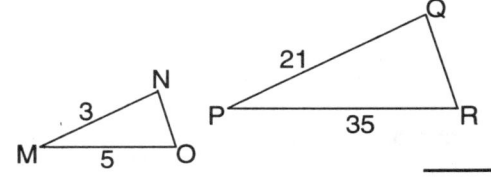

4. Right triangles ABC and DEF are similar. In $\triangle$ABC the lengths of the legs are 6 and 8. In $\triangle$DEF the length of the shorter leg is 24. What is the length of the longer leg of $\triangle$DEF?

5. The lengths of the sides of $\triangle$DEF are 12, 9 and 8. The longest side of similar triangle QRS is 60. Find the length of the shortest side of $\triangle$QRS.

6. If the ratio of the corresponding sides of two similar triangles is 2:7, the ratio of the areas of these triangles is:
   (1) 2:7   (3) 4:49
   (2) $\sqrt{2}:\sqrt{7}$ (4) 4:14

7. If the ratio of the corresponding sides of two similar triangles is 4:25, the ratio of the perimeters of these triangles is:
   (1) 4:25   (3) 2:5
   (2) 16:625   (4) 5:2

8. In the accompanying diagram $\triangle$MNO is similar to $\triangle$PQR. $\angle M \cong \angle P$ and $\angle N \cong \angle Q$. If PQ = 21, MN = 3, PR = 35 and MO = 5, how many times larger is side QR than side NO?

9. The ratio of Tom's shadow to Emily's shadow is 2:1. If Tom is 5 feet tall, how tall is Emily?

10. A pole casts a shadow of 30 feet long at the same time a man 6 feet tall casts a shadow 4 feet long. Find the number of feet in the height of the pole.

Chapter 5
ANGLES & TRIANGLES
Chapter Test

1. Two supplementary angles are in the ratio of 5:31. Find the number of degrees in the smallest angle.

2. The three angles of a triangle are in the ratio of 12:5:1. Find the number of degrees in the largest angle of the triangle.

3. In the accompanying diagram, △ABC is a right triangle with AB = 17 and BC = 15. Find AC.

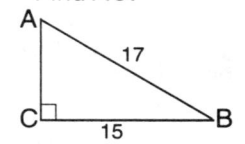

4. In △ABC, m∠A = 65 and the m∠B = 75. Find the m∠ACD.

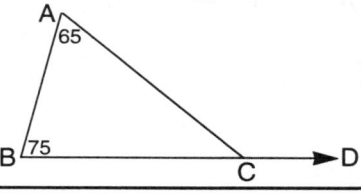

5. In the accompanying diagram, △ABC is similar △DEF. If AB = 5, BC = 6, AC = 3 and DE = 10, find DF.

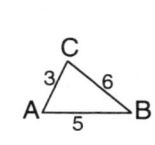

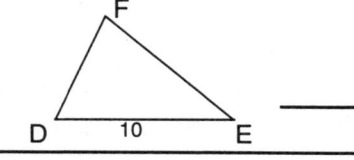

6. In the diagram below, $\overleftrightarrow{AB}$ || $\overleftrightarrow{CD}$. If the m∠1 = (5x−20) and the m∠2 = (3x+10), find m∠1.

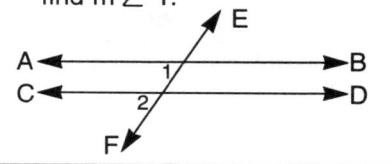

7. If the measure of one base angle of an isosceles triangle is 37, find the value of the vertex angle.
   (1) 37   (3) 143
   (2) 106   (4) 53

8. In the accompanying diagram, $\overleftrightarrow{ABC}$ is a straight line, $\overrightarrow{BD} \perp \overrightarrow{BE}$, and m∠CBE = 25. Find m∠ABD.

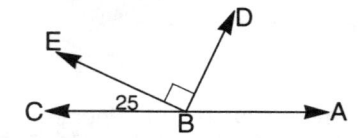

9. Two complementary angles are in the ratio 7:3. The number of degrees in the *larger* angle is:
   (1) 9   (3) 63
   (2) 27   (4) 70

10. If the ratio of the corresponding sides of two similar triangles is 2:1, the ratio of the areas of these triangles is:
    (1) 2:1   (3) 1:2
    (2) $\sqrt{2}$: 1   (4) 4:1

11. In the accompanying diagram, $\overleftrightarrow{AB}$ is parallel to $\overleftrightarrow{CD}$, m∠BAC = 30, and m∠BCD = 80. Find the measure of ∠ACB.

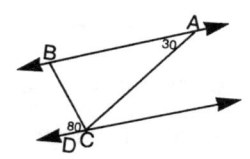

12. Two vertical angles are represented by (4x+20) and (2x+40). Find the value of x.
    (1) 10   (3) 30
    (2) 20   (4) 40

Chapter 5
ANGLES & TRIANGLES
Chapter Test (Continued)

13. Two supplementary angles are in the ratio 5:4. The number of degrees in the larger angle is:

    (1) 10   (3) 80
    (2) 20   (4) 100

14. What is the supplement of an angle that measures 2x?

    (1) 2x - 90   (3) 2x - 180
    (2) 90 - 2x   (4) 180 - 2x

15. In the accompanying diagram, $\overleftrightarrow{AOB}$ is a straight line, m∠AOD = 6x-20 and m∠BOD = 2x. What is the value of x?

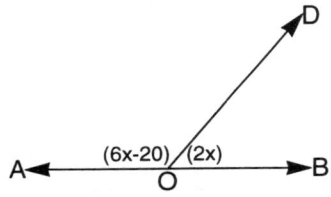

16. Two angles are supplementary. If one of these angles measures 40 less than the other, find the measure of the larger angle.

17. In the accompanying diagram, $\overrightarrow{DH}$ ∥ $\overline{EF}$. If m∠HDF = 28 and m∠EDF = 60, find m∠E.

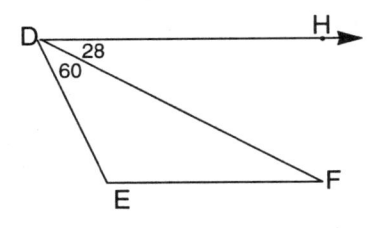

18. In the accompanying diagram of △ABC, the measure of exterior angle BCD is 120 and m∠BAC = 40. Find m∠ABC.

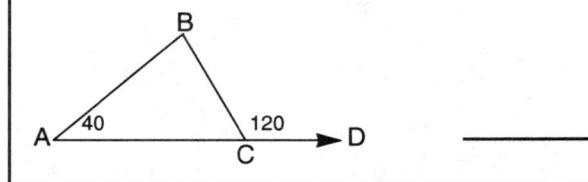

19. If the angles of a triangle are represented by x, 3x-30 and 3x, the triangle must be:

    (1) acute   (3) obtuse
    (2) isosceles   (4) right

20. A wire reaches from the top of a 16 meter telephone pole to a point on the ground 7 meters from the base of the pole. What is the length of the wire to the *nearest tenth* of a meter?

21. In the accompanying diagram, $\overline{CD}$ is the bisector of ∠ACB, m∠A = 32 and m∠B = 64. Find m∠BCD.

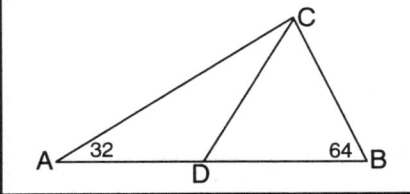

22. Two angles are complementary. If one of these angles measures 10 more than the other, find the measure of the smaller angle.

67

Chapter 6
GEOMETRIC CONCEPTS

Perimeter and Area

> **REMEMBER**
> Important formulas to remember are:
>
> - The Perimeter of any geometric figure = the sum of all of its sides.
> $$(P = a + b + c + ...)$$
>
> - The Area of a square or rectangle = the base times the height.
> $$(A = bh)$$
>
> - The Area of a triangle = one-half the product of the base and the height (or altitude).
> $$(A = \tfrac{1}{2}bh)$$
>
> **Example:** The side of square is represented by (x+5). Express the area of the square in terms of x.
>
> $A = bh$
> $A = (x+5)(x+5)$
> $A = x^2 + 10x + 25$ Ans.

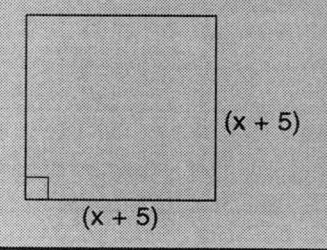

1. If s represents the side of a square, represent the perimeter in terms of s.

2. If p represents the perimeter of a square, represent the length of a side of the square in terms of p.

3. A rectangle has an area of 40 square meters. If the width is 5 meters, what is the length, in meters, of the rectangle?

4. The side of a square is (x+2). Express the perimeter of the square in terms of x.

5. The length of a rectangle is represented by x. If the width of the rectangle is 4 less than its length, which expression represents the area of the rectangle.
   (1) x(x - 4)   (3) 2x - 8
   (2) x^2 - 4   (4) 2x + 8

6. The area of a rectangle is represented by $x^2 + x - 6$. If the width of the rectangle is represented by (x - 2), the length may be represented by:
   (1) (x - 3)   (3) x + 4
   (2) (x + 3)   (4) (x - 4)

68

Chapter 6
GEOMETRIC CONCEPTS

Perimeter and Area (Continued)

7. The perimeter of square is represented by (4x + 16). Express the length of one side of the square in terms of x.

8. The measures of the sides of a triangle can be represented by (2a - 5), (3a + 4) and (5a - 7). Express the perimeter of the triangle as a binomial in terms of a.

9. The area of a triangle is 30 square meters and the base measures 10 meters. Find the number of meters in the measure of the altitude.

10. The length and width of a rectangle are represented by (x + 9) and (x - 5). If the area of the rectangle is 60, which equation can be used to find x?
    (1) (x-5) + (x+9) = 60
    (2) (x-5) - (x+9) = 60
    (3) 2(x-5) + 2(x+9) = 60
    (4) (x+9) (x-5) = 60

11. A rectangle has an area of 16. If the length of the rectangle is doubled and the width remains the same, what is the area of the new rectangle?

12. If both the base and height of a triangle are doubled, the area of the triangle will be multiplied by:
    (1) $\frac{1}{2}$ (3) $\frac{1}{4}$
    (2) 2   (4) 4

13. The length of a rectangle is four times its width. If the width is represented by x, which expression represents the perimeter of the rectangle?
    (1) 5x   (3) 10x
    (2) $4x^2$ (4) 4x + 8

14. A triangle has a base of 12 centimeters and an area of 24 square centimeters. What is the height of the triangle?
    (1) 6 cm   (3) 3 cm
    (2) 2 cm   (4) 4 cm

15. In the accompanying diagram the lengths of the sides of the quadrilateral are represented by x, 3x, (2x-5) and (3x+2). Express the perimeter as a binomial in terms of x.

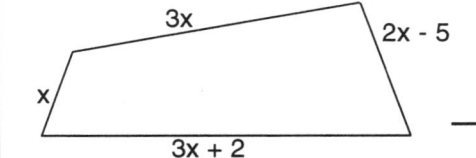

16. If the length of a rectangle is doubled and its width is multiplied by five, the area of the rectangle is multiplied by:
    (1) 10   (3) 8
    (2) 2   (4) 5

Chapter 6
GEOMETRIC CONCEPTS

Perimeter and Area (Continued)

17. A rectangle has an area of $x^2 - 9$. If the length of the rectangle is represented by $(x+3)$, express its width in terms of x.

    _____

18. If the perimeter of a square is 48, find the area of the square.

    _____

19. If the area of a square is 36, find the perimeter of the square.

    _____

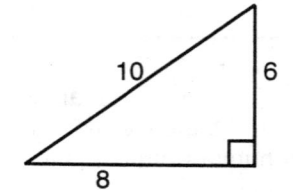

20. The length of a rectangle is represented by $(x+7)$ and the width by $(x-3)$. The area of the rectangle is represented by:

    (1) $2x + 4$ (3) $x^2 + 4x - 21$
    (2) $x^2 - 21$ (4) $4x + 8$

    _____

21. If the width of a rectangle is 9 less than the length, represent the perimeter of the rectangle as a binomial in terms of x.

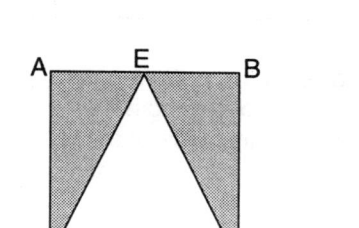

    _____

22. Each side of a regular pentagon is represented by $2x$. Represent the perimeter in terms of x.

    _____

23. If each side of a regular hexagon is represented by $(x+6)$, which expression represents the perimeter of the hexagon?

    (1) $6x + 36$ (3) $8x + 48$
    (2) $6x + 6$ (4) $42x$

    _____

24. The area of the right triangle drawn below is:

    (1) 24
    (2) 40
    (3) 48
    (4) 60

    _____

25. If the length of a rectangle is 9 more than the width, the area of the rectangle can be represented by:

    (1) $x^2 + 9$ (3) $x^2 + 9x$
    (2) $9x^2$ (4) $2x + 9$

    _____

26. In the accompanying diagram, triangle DEC is inscribed in square ABCD. If the length of side DC is 8, what is the area of the shaded portion of the diagram?

    _____

Chapter 6
GEOMETRIC CONCEPTS

Parallelograms

REMEMBER

Important properties of parallelograms:

- Opposite sides are parallel.
- Opposite sides are congruent.
- Opposite angles are congruent.
- Consecutive angles are supplementary.
- Diagonals bisect each other.

Example: In the accompanying figure, ABCD is a parallelogram, AB = 25, CD = 10x - 5. Find the value of x.

Solution: 10x - 5 = 25
10x = 30
x = 3 Ans.

---

1. Which property is *not* common to all parallelograms?

   (1) Opposite angles are congruent
   (2) Consecutive angles are complementary
   (3) Opposite sides are congruent
   (4) Opposite sides are parallel

2. In the accompanying figure, ABCD is a parallelogram, m∠A = 3x + 2, and m∠C = 6x - 61. Find the value of x.

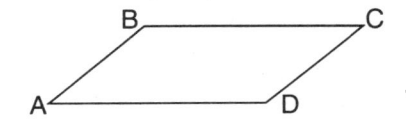

3. In parallelogram ABCD, the measure of angle ABC is 165 degrees. Find the measure in degrees of angle C.

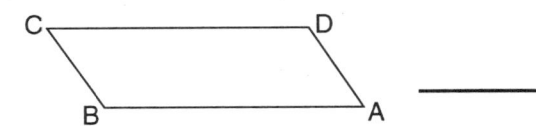

4. A quadrilateral with four congruent sides and an angle measuring 75 degrees must be a:

   (1) square   (3) trapezoid
   (2) rhombus   (4) rectangle

5. In the accompanying figure, ABCD is a parallelogram. Which statement must be true?

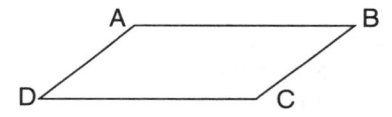

   (1) Angles A and D are congruent
   (2) Angles A and D are supplementary
   (3) Angles A and D are complementary
   (4) The sum of the measures of the four angles is 180 degrees

6. In parallelogram ABCD, AB = 41 and DC = 6x-7. Find the value of x.

7. In parallelogram ABCD, diagonals $\overline{AC}$ and $\overline{BD}$ intersect at E. If DE = 27 and EB = 5x + 7. Find the value of x.

8. In parallelogram ABCD, m∠A = 7x+16 and m∠D = 2x-7. Find the number of degrees in ∠A.

Chapter 6
GEOMETRIC CONCEPTS

Volume

REMEMBER

Important formulas to remember are:

- Volume of a Rectangular Solid: $V = lwh$ (length times width times height)
- Volume of a Cube: $V = e^3$ (Edge cubed)

Example: Find the volume of a cube with an edge of 3.

$$V = e^3$$
$$V = 3^3 \quad (3 \times 3 \times 3)$$
$$V = 27 \text{ Ans.}$$

1. The length of the edge of a cube is 6. Find the volume of the cube.

2. Express in cubic feet, the volume of a room whose dimensions are 15 feet long by 10 feet wide by 9 feet high.

3. The length of an edge of a cube is represented by 4x. Which expression represents the volume of the cube?
   (1) $8x^2$ (3) $4x^3$
   (2) $16x^2$ (4) $64x^3$

4. Find the volume of a rectangular solid whose length is 20 feet, width is 12 feet and whose height is 8 feet.

5. If the side of a cube is doubled, the volume is multiplied by:
   (1) 6   (3) 8
   (2) 2   (4) 4

6. If the length, width and height of a rectangular solid are each doubled, then the volume of the original figured is multiplied by a factor of:
   (1) 16   (3) 8
   (2) 2   (4) 4

7. The length of an edge of a cube is represented by x. Express the volume of the cube in terms of x.

8. A rectangular box has dimensions of 4 by 3 by 2. Find the volume of the box.

9. What is the length of an edge of a cube that has a volume of 1000 cubic feet?
   (1) 10 feet   (3) 1000 feet
   (2) 100 feet   (4) 50 feet

10. Find the height of a rectangular solid whose volume is 378, length is 9 and width is 7.

Chapter 6
GEOMETRIC CONCEPTS
The Circumference and Area of a Circle

REMEMBER

Important formulas to remember:

Circumference of a Circle = $C = \pi D$ or $C = 2\pi R$

Area of a Circle = $A = \pi R^2$

Example: The circumference of a circle is 10π. What is the area of the circle?

First find C: $C = 2\pi R$
$10\pi = 2\pi R$
$5 = R$

Then: $A = \pi R^2$
$A = \pi 5^2$
$A = 25\pi$ Ans.

---

1. The circumference of a circle is 14π. What is the radius of the circle?

2. If the area of circle is 16π, the circumference of the circle is:
   (1) 8π (3) 4π
   (2) 8   (4) 4

3. The circumference of a circle is 40π. What is the area of the circle?
   (1) 20π (3) 1600
   (2) 400π (4) 1600π

4. What is the diameter of a circle whose circumference is equal to 20π?

5. Find the area of a circle whose circumference is equal to 8π.

6. The circumference of a circle is represented by $2\pi R$. If the radius of the circle is doubled, then the circumference is:
   (1) multiplied by 4   (3) squared
   (2) increased by 2   (4) doubled

7. As shown in the accompanying diagram, a square with side s is inscribed in a circle with radius r. Which expression represents the area of the shaded region?

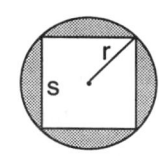

   (1) $s^2 - \pi r^2$ (3) $\pi r^2 - 4s$
   (2) $\pi r^2 - s^2$ (4) $4s - \pi r^2$

Chapter 6
GEOMETRIC CONCEPTS
Finding the Slope of a Line Passing Through Two Points

REMEMBER

To find the slope of a line passing through two points, use the formula $m = \frac{y_2 - y_1}{x_2 - x_1}$ where m = the slope and (x_1, y_1) and (x_2, y_2) are the points.

Example: Find the slope of the line passing through the points (3,4) and (5,9).

$m = \frac{y_2 - y_1}{x_2 - x_1}$ (3,4) (5,9)
   (x_1,y_1) (x_2,y_2)

$m = \frac{9 - 4}{5 - 3}$ $m = \frac{5}{2}$ ans.

---

1. What is the slope of the line determined by the points (3,1) and (4,2)?

2. The graph of the line passing through the points (5,-2) and (3,5) has a slope of:
   (1) $-\frac{2}{7}$ (3) $-\frac{2}{3}$
   (2) $-\frac{7}{2}$ (4) $-\frac{3}{2}$

3. Find the slope of the line passing through the points (4,6) and (6,9).

4. Which of the following pairs of points could determine a line whose slope equals $\frac{1}{2}$?
   (1) (5,0) (-5,10)   (3) (1,-1) (9,3)
   (2) (3,3) (6,6)   (4) (3,-2) (7,6)

5. The graph of the line passing through the points (0,-2) and (3,0) has a slope of:
   (1) $-\frac{2}{3}$ (3) $\frac{2}{3}$
   (2) $-\frac{3}{2}$ (4) $\frac{3}{2}$

6. Find the slope of the line determined by the points (-4,8) and (-6,2).

7. (True or False) The slope of a line passing through the points (-1,1) and (3,-3) is -1.

8. The graph of the line passing through the points (7,2) and (9,8) has a slope of:
   (1) $\frac{5}{8}$ (3) 3
   (2) $\frac{8}{5}$ (4) $\frac{1}{3}$

Chapter 6
GEOMETRIC CONCEPTS

Equation of a Line

> **REMEMBER**
> The standard form for the equation of a line is y = mx + b where m equals the slope and b equals the y-intercept. Lines that are parallel have slopes that are equal.
>
> **Example:** Write the equation of a line that has a slope of $\frac{1}{2}$ and a y intercept of 5.
>
> Slope y - intercept form: $\quad y = mx + b$
> Replace m with $\frac{1}{2}$ and b with 5: $y = \frac{1}{2}x + 5$ Ans.

1. The line whose equation is $y = \frac{1}{3}x + 4$ has a slope of:

   (1) 1   (3) 3
   (2) $\frac{1}{3}$ (4) 4

2. The graph of which equation has a slope of 4?

   (1) y = 4x - 3   (3) y = -4x + 3
   (2) y = 3x - 4   (4) y = -3x + 4

3. Which is the equation of a line parallel to the line whose equation is y = 2x + 3?

   (1) $y = -\frac{1}{2}x + 3$ (3) y = 2x - 3
   (2) $y = \frac{1}{2}x + 3$ (4) y = -2x - 3

4. Find the slope of the line whose equation is y = -9x + 8.

   (1) -9   (3) 9
   (2) 8   (4) -8

5. Write the equation of a line with a slope of 6 and a y-intercept of -7.

   (1) y = 7x - 6   (3) y = -6x + 7
   (2) y = -7x + 6   (4) y = 6x - 7

6. One line is parallel to another line whose slope is $\frac{1}{3}$. If the y-intercept of the first line is 4, what is the equation of that line?

7. What is the slope of a line parallel to the line whose equation is y = 5x + 4?

   (1) $-\frac{5}{4}$ (3) $-\frac{4}{5}$
   (2) 5   (4) 4

8. A line has a slope of -1 and a y-intercept of 3. An equation of the line is:

   (1) y = 3x - 1   (3) y = -x + 3
   (2) y = -3x + 1   (4) y = -x - 3

Chapter 6
GEOMETRIC CONCEPTS

Equations of Special Lines

REMEMBER

A line passing through the point (2,3) and parallel to the x-axis will have an equation of y = 3. (The y coordinate)

A line passing through the point (2,3) and parallel to the y-axis will have an equation of x = 2. (The x coordinate)

---

1. An equation of the line which is parallel to the x-axis and 4 units below the x-axis is:
   (1) y = -4   (3) x = 4
   (2) y = 4   (4) x = -4

2. What is the point of intersection of the graphs x = 2 and y = 4?
   (1) (2,4)   (3) (-2,4)
   (2) (4,2)   (4) (-4,2)

3. The graph of the equation y = 6 intersects the y-axis at the point whose coordinates are:
   (1) (-6,6)   (3) (6,0)
   (2) (0,6)   (4) (6,6)

4. Write the equation of the line parallel to the x-axis and 7 units above it.
   (1) x = 7   (3) y = 7
   (2) x = -7   (4) y = -7

5. When drawn on the same set of axes, the graphs of the equations y = -3 and x = 5 intersect at the point whose coordinates are:
   (1) (-3,5)   (3) (5,-3)
   (2) (3,-5)   (4) (-3,5)

6. Write the equation of the line parallel to the y-axis and 1 unit to the left of it.

7. The graphs of the lines x = 7 and y = -2 intersect at the point whose coordinates are:
   (1) (7,-2)   (3) (-7,2)
   (2) (-2,7)   (4) (2,-7)

8. What is another name for the line whose equation is y = 0?

9. The intersection of y = 3 and the y axis has the coordinates:
   (1) (3,0)   (3) (-3,0)
   (2) (0,3)   (4) (0,-3)

76

Chapter 6
GEOMETRIC CONCEPTS

Points on a Line

REMEMBER

If a point lies on the graph of a line, its coordinates will satisfy the equation of that line.

Example: Which point does not lie on the graph of x - 3y = 15?

(1) (0,-5)   (3) (5,0)
(2) (6,-3)   (4) (9,-2)

Substituting each point in the equation, the only one that does not satisfy the equation is the point (5,0).

$$x - 3y = 15$$
$$5 - 3(0) = 15$$
$$5 - 0 = 15$$
$$5 \neq 15 \text{ Does not satisfy the equation}$$

---

1. Which point does not lie on the graph of the equation 3x + y = 2?
   (1) (1,-1)   (3) (2,-4)
   (2) (-1,1)   (4) (0,2)

2. If the point (3,2) lies on the graph of the equation 2x + ky = -4, find the value of k.

3. If (a,-3) is a point on the graph of the equation 3x + y = 9, what is the value of a?
   (1) -4   (3) 3
   (2) 9   (4) 4

4. If the point (2,1) lies on the graph of the equation kx + 2y = 8, find the value of k.

5. What are the coordinates of the y-intercept for the equation y - 3x = 6?
   (1) (0,-6)   (3) (0,3)
   (2) (0,6)   (4) (0,-3)

6. The point whose coordinates are (4,k) lies on the line whose equations is y = 5x - 2. Find the value of k.

7. If point (k,-1) lies on the graph of the equation 2x - 3y = 5, what is the value of k?
   (1) 1   (3) -3
   (2) -1   (4) 4

8. The graph of 3x + y = 5 contains the point:
   (1) (1,2)   (3) (2,1)
   (2) (-2,1)   (4) (-1,2)

9. Which point satisfies the inequality 3x + y > 7?
   (1) (1,3)   (3) (2,1)
   (2) (0,6)   (4) (4,-2)

10. Which point does not lie on the graph of the equation 2x + y = 5?
    (1) ($\frac{1}{2}$,4)   (3) (2,1)
    (2) (1,2)   (4) (3,-1)

77

Chapter 6
GEOMETRIC CONCEPTS

Coordinate Geometry

REMEMBER

Example: In the accompanying figure, △ABC has coordinates A (2,2), B (6,2) and C (6,6). Find the area of △ABC
(1) 18 (3) 16
(2) 8 (4) 36

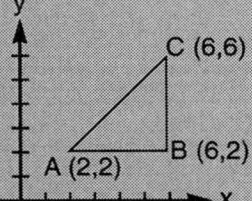

Solution:
$A = \frac{1}{2}bh = \frac{1}{2}(\overline{AB})(\overline{BC})$
$A = \frac{1}{2}(4)(4) = 8$
Ans. = (2)

---

1. In the accompanying diagram, square ABCD has vertices A(0,0), B(a+1,0), C(a+1,a+1) and D(0,a+1). What is the area of square ABCD?

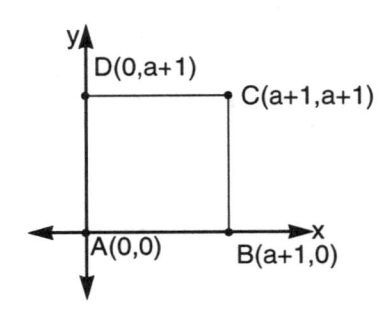

   (1) 4a + 4   (3) a^2 + 1
   (2) 2a + 2   (4) a^2 + 2a + 1

2. In the accompanying figure, △ABC has coordinates A(0,3), B(6,3) and C(0,6). Find the area of △ABC.

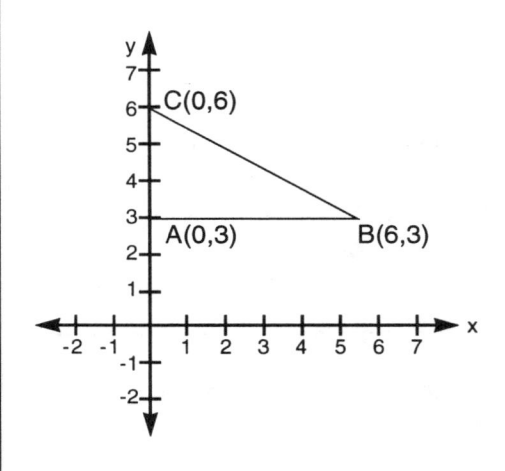

3. In the accompanying diagram, rectangle ABCD has vertices A(0,0), B(5,0), C(5,b) and D(0,b). What is the area of rectangle ABCD?

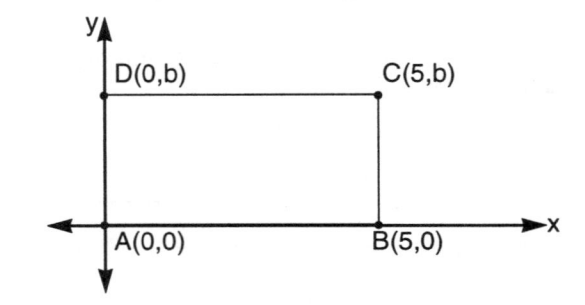

   (1) 5b   (3) 10 + 2b
   (2) 5 + b (4) $25b^2$

4. Find the area of a square ABCD with vertices A(-4,4), B(4,4), C(4,-4) and D(-4,-4).

5. Find the area of a rectangle QRST with vertices Q(-4,5), R(2,5), S(2,-3) and T(-4,-3).

78

Chapter 6
GEOMETRIC CONCEPTS

Graphs of Inequalities

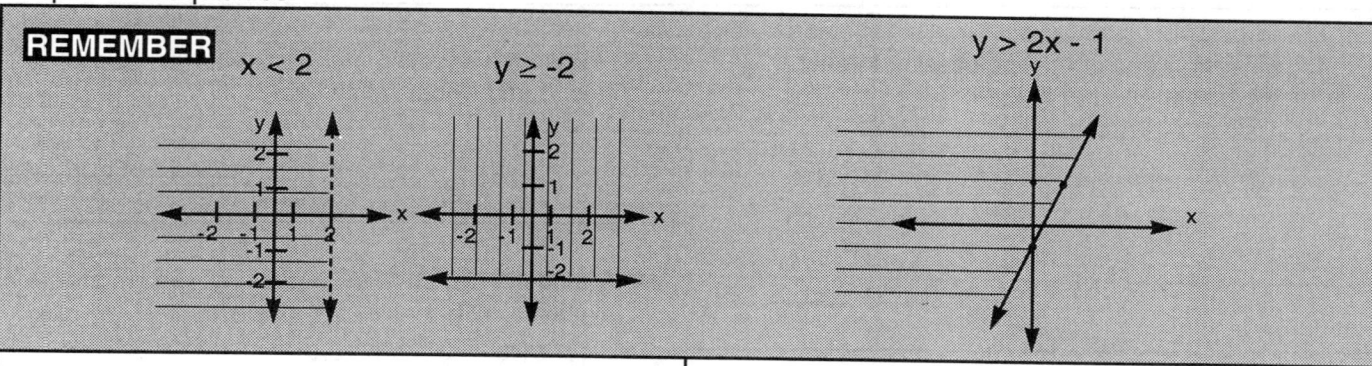

REMEMBER $x < 2$ $y \geq -2$ $y > 2x - 1$

1. Which diagram below represents the graph of the statement $x \leq 3$?

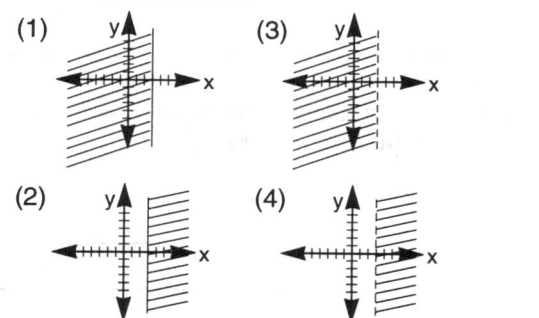

   (1)   (2)   (3)   (4)

2. The graph of which inequality is shown in the accompanying diagram?

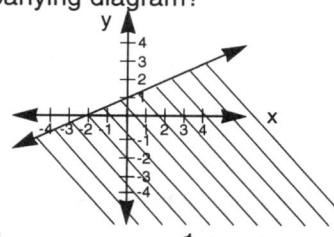

   (1) $y \geq \frac{1}{2}x + 1$ (3) $y \leq \frac{1}{2}x + 1$
   (2) $y > \frac{1}{2}x + 1$ (4) $y < \frac{1}{2}x + 1$

3. Which diagram below represents the graph of the statement $x > 3$?

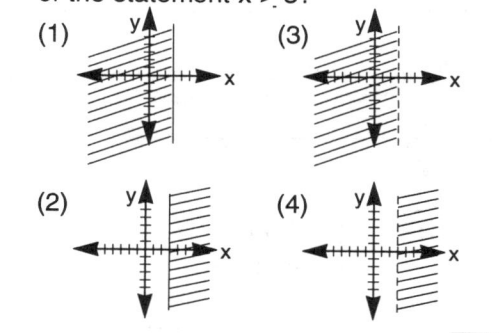

   (1)   (2)   (3)   (4)

4. Which ordered pair is not in the solution set of the system of inequalities shown in the accompanying graph?

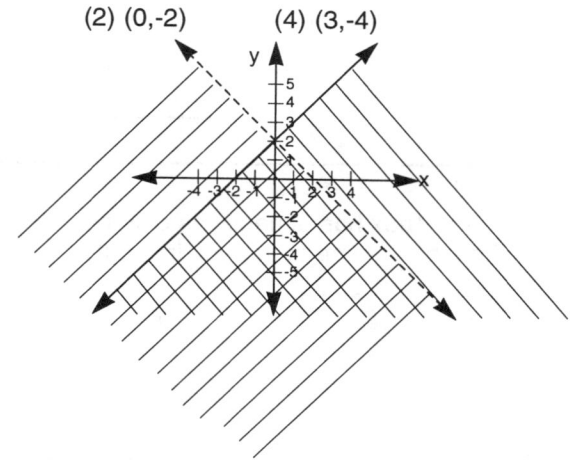

   (1) (-2,0)   (3) (2,0)
   (2) (0,-2)   (4) (3,-4)

5. Which ordered pair is in the solution set of the system of inequalities show in the accompanying diagram?

   (1) (5,2)   (3) (1,-5)
   (2) (2,0)   (4) (-5,2)

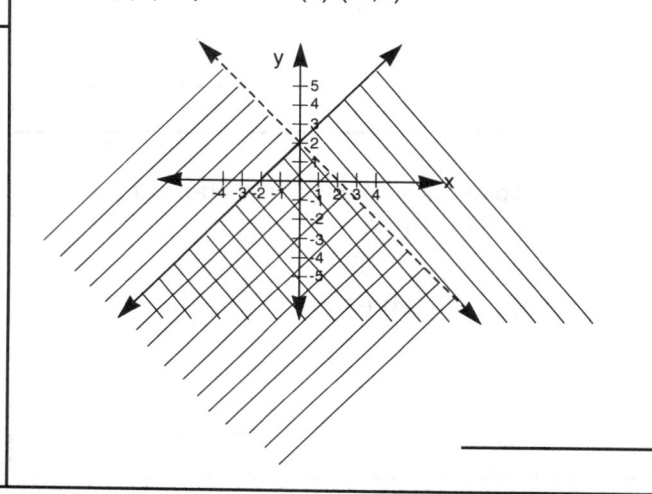

79

Chapter 6
GEOMETRIC CONCEPTS
Chapter Test

1. Find the slope of the line passing through the points (9,-1) and (7,4).

2. The area of a triangle is 80 square meters and the base measures 20 meters. Find the number of meters in the measure of the altitude.

3. A rectangular box has dimensions of 8' by 7' by 4'. Find the volume of the box in cu. ft.

4. Find the perimeter of a square whose area is equal to 64 square meters.
   (1) 128　　(3) 32
   (2) 64　　(4) 8

5. Which point does not lie on the graph of the equation 3x - y = 2?
   (1) (4,8)　　(3) (3,7)
   (2) (1,1)　　(4) (-1,-5)

6. Write the equation of the line whose slope is -6 and whose y-intercept is 3.

7. Find the circumference of a circle whose area equals 81π.
   (1) 81π　　(3) 18π
   (2) 9π　　(4) 162π

8. Write the equation of the line passing through the point (-6,8) and parallel to the x-axis.

9. In the accompanying figure, ABCD is a parallelogram. Which statement must be true?

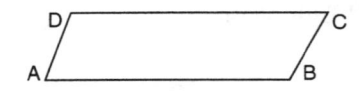

   (1) Angle A is 90 degrees
   (2) If angle B = 150, angle D = 30
   (3) If angle C = 75, angle B = 285
   (4) If angle D = 175, angle A = 5

10. In the accompanying diagram, rectangle ABCD has vertices A(0,0), B(0,q+1), C(t,q+1) and D(t,0). What is the area of rectangle ABCD?:

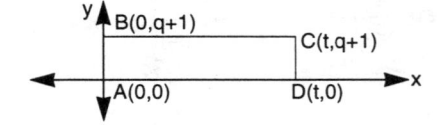

    (1) 2t+2q+2　　(3) t(q+1)
    (2) t^2　　(4) q^2+2q+1

Chapter 6
GEOMETRIC CONCEPTS
Chapter Test (Continued)

11. Which ordered pair is in the solution set of the system of inequalities shown in the accompanying graph?

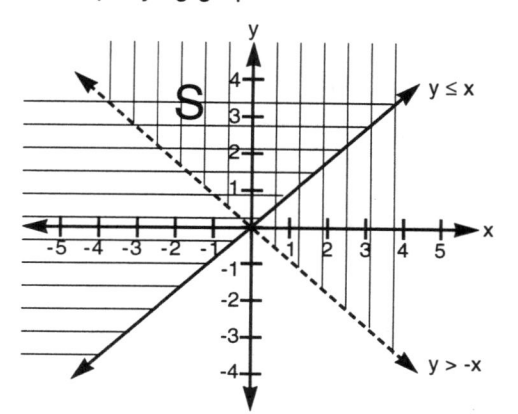

(1) (-4,0) (3) (4,0)
(2) (0,-4) (4) (0,4)

12. Find the volume of a cube whose edge is 3x.
(1) $9x^2$ (3) $27x$
(2) $12x$ (4) $27x^3$

13. Find the area of a circle whose circumference is equal to 12π.

14. If in parallelogram ABCD, m∠A = 73, find the m∠B.

15. Which ordered pair is not in the solution set of the system of inequalities show in the accompanying graph?

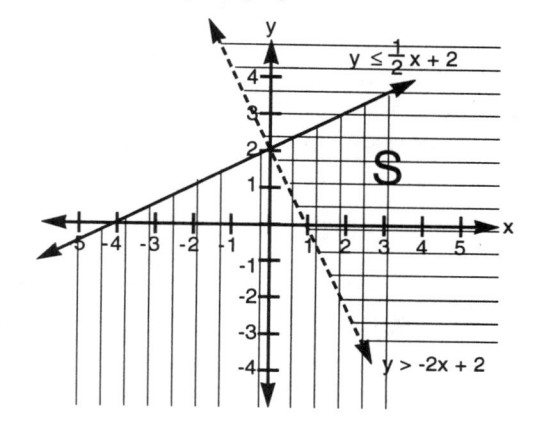

(1) (0,2) (3) (4,2)
(2) (2,0) (4) (4,-2)

16. Write the equation of a line parallel to the x-axis and passing through the point (-3,2).
(1) y = 2 (3) y = -3
(2) x = 2 (4) x = -3

17. If the opposite sides of a parallelogram are represented by 3x + 18 and 5x + 6, find the value of x.

18. Which inequality is represented by the graph below?

(1) $-1 < x \leq 2$ (3) $-1 \leq x \leq 2$
(2) $-1 \leq x < 2$ (4) $-1 < x < 2$

81

Chapter 7
PROBABILITY AND STATISTICS

Counting Principle

> **REMEMBER**
> If there are 5 ways an event can occur and 11 ways a second event can occur, then the total number of ways both events can occur is (5) (11) = 55 ways.

1. There are 9 roads from Oz to Dor and 7 roads from Dor to Zeb. How many different roads could be driven from Oz to Zeb?
   (1) 9   (3) 16
   (2) 63   (4) 81

2. A lottery consists of selecting one out of 10 colors and one out of 50 numbers. How many different tickets can be sold consisting of one color and one number?

3. If 2 dice are tossed simultaneously, how many outcomes are possible?

4. John rents one of the top 12 video's and one of the top 4 albums. How many different rentals consisting of one video and one album can John rent?

5. A bag has 5 red balls, 8 blue balls and 4 yellow balls. Picking 3 balls at a time, how many different results can occur?

6. If a card is picked from a standard deck of cards and a coin is tossed, how many different outcomes are possible?
   (1) 8   (3) 54
   (2) 52   (4) 104

7. Funland has 15 rides, 6 shows and 3 restaurants. How many ways can Tommy spend the day if he selects one ride, one show and one restaurant?
   (1) 270   (3) 45
   (2) 24   (4) 21

8. In a class of 30 students, 10 are fourteen years old, 18 are fifteen years old and 2 are sixteen years old. How many 3 member teams can be formed consisting of one student from each age group?
   (1) 50   (3) 1080
   (2) 360   (4) 2500

9. If Jose has 8 shirts, 3 pairs of slacks and 2 pairs of shoes, how many different outfits consisting of one shirt, one pair of slacks and one pair of shoes can Jose wear?
   (1) 13   (3) 144
   (2) 16   (4) 48

Chapter 7
PROBABILITY AND STATISTICS

Factorial, Permutations

> **REMEMBER**
>
> Factorial (!) as in 5! means (5)(4)(3)(2)(1) = 120
>
> $$_nP_r = \frac{n!}{(n-r)!} \qquad _7P_3 = \frac{7!}{(7-3)!} = \frac{(7)(6)(5)(4)(3)(2)(1)}{(4)(3)(2)(1)} = 210$$
>
> **Example:** How many three-digit numbers can be formed from the digits 4, 6, and 8? (Each digit can only be used once) **Reminder:** 0! = 1
>
> $$_3P_3 = \frac{3!}{(3-3)!} = \frac{(3)(2)(1)}{1} = 6$$

1. Evaluate:

   (a) 4! _____   (b) $\frac{7!}{5!}$ _____

   (c) $_5P_3$ _____   (d) $\frac{10!}{7!}$ _____

2. What is the number of possible 4-letter arrangements of the letters W, X, Y, Z if each letter is used only once in each arrangement?

3. In how many different ways can a history book, an English book, a math book, a comic book and a physics book be arranged on a shelf?

4. In how many different ways can 6 students be arranged in 6 seats?

5. How many 3-digit numbers can be formed from the digits of 3, 4, 5, and 6 if a digit can appear just once in a number?

6. The value of $_6P_2$ is:

   (1) 6   (3) 30
   (2) 12   (4) 720

7. How many 2-digit numbers can be made using the digits 2, 3, 4, 5, 9 if each digit is used just once in each number?

8. In how many different ways can art, music, math and health be scheduled during the first four periods of the day?

9. In how many different ways can 12 students be seated in 2 seats?

10. How many arrangements of 4 letters can be formed from V, I, D, E, O if each letter is used exactly once in each arrangement?

Chapter 7
PROBABILITY AND STATISTICS

Simple Probability

> **REMEMBER**
> The probability of an event $P(E) = \dfrac{\text{Number of successful outcomes}}{\text{Number of total outcomes}}$

1. If all nine letters of the word "CHOCOLATE" were placed in a pot, what would be the probability of drawing an O at random on the first draw? _____

2. If a number is picked at random from the set {-2, -1, 0, 1, 2}, what is the probability that the number satisfies the equation $x^2 - 4 = 0$? _____

3. A single six-sided die is rolled. What is the probability of rolling:
   (a) an even number? _____
   (b) an odd number? _____
   (c) a number greater than 4? _____
   (d) a seven? _____

4. A single card is drawn at random from a standard 52 card deck. What is the probability of drawing:
   (a) a king? _____
   (b) an ace of clubs? _____
   (c) a red card? _____
   (d) a face card? _____
   (e) less than 5? _____
   (f) a heart? _____
   (g) a red 8? _____

5. On a game show the $10,000 prize is hidden in one of 5 boxes. What is the probability of selecting the box containing the $10,000 prize? _____

6. There are 13 boys and 16 girls in a math class. If the teacher calls on a student at random, what is the probability that the student called is a boy?
   (1) $\dfrac{13}{29}$ (3) $\dfrac{16}{29}$
   (2) $\dfrac{13}{16}$ (4) $\dfrac{1}{2}$
   _____

7. A purse contains 5 pennies, 6 dimes and 8 quarters. If one coin is drawn at random from the purse, what is the probability that it is NOT a dime? _____

8. A single card is drawn at random from a standard deck of 52 cards. Which event has the largest probability of occurring?
   (1) drawing a red card
   (2) drawing a club
   (3) drawing a king
   (4) drawing a face card
   _____

9. If a number is picked at random from the set {-4, -3, -2, -1, 0, 1, 2, 3, 4}, what is the probability that the number satisfies the inequality $x + 4 > 6$? _____

10. A letter is chosen at random from the letters of the word "FREEDOM". What is the probability that the letter chosen is a consonant? _____

Chapter 7
PROBABILITY AND STATISTICS
P (certain event), P (impossible event), Sample space

REMEMBER

P (certain event) = 1   P (impossible event) = 0
P (A) + P (not A) = 1 that is the probability has to be between 0 and 1.

To find the probability of throwing an 8 on a pair of dice, look at the sample space (possible outcomes) at the right and see how many have the sum of 8. Divide this sum by the total outcomes. Ans. $\frac{5}{36}$

	Red Die					
	1	2	3	4	5	6
Green Die 1	2	3	4	5	6	7
2	3	4	5	6	7	8
3	4	5	6	7	8	9
4	5	6	7	8	9	10
5	6	7	8	9	10	11
6	7	8	9	10	11	12

1. A single-die is tossed once. What is the probability of getting a number less than 8?

   _____

2. If the probability of an event NOT happening is $\frac{3}{10}$, what is the probability that the event will happen?

   _____

3. The weather bureau predicts a 45% chance of rain. What is the probability that it will not rain?

   _____

4. If the probability that SeaWest will win a soccer game is $\frac{2}{3}$, what is the probability that they will NOT win the game?

   _____

5. If the probability that Damien wins the election is 0.7, what is the probability that Damien will not win the election?

   _____

6. In a single toss of two dice, what is the probability of attaining the same number of each die?

   _____

7. The probability of an event is represented by P(E). Which is a true statement?

   (1) $0 \leq P(E) \leq 1$ (3) $0 < P(E) \leq 1$
   (2) $0 < P(E) < 1$ (4) $0 \leq P(E) < 1$

   _____

8. On a test the probability of getting the correct answer to a question is $\frac{x}{4}$. Which cannot be a value of x?

   (1) 1   (3) 0
   (2) -1   (4) 4

   _____

9. If 2 six-sided dice are rolled, what is the probability of getting a sum of 3?

   (1) $\frac{1}{36}$ (3) $\frac{3}{36}$
   (2) $\frac{2}{36}$ (4) $\frac{2}{6}$

   _____

10. If a pair of dice is rolled, what is the probability of getting a sum of:
    (a) four _____
    (b) eight _____
    (c) thirteen _____
    (d) one _____
    (e) seven _____

Chapter 7
PROBABILITY AND STATISTICS

Events A and B

REMEMBER

Example 1: What is the probability of picking a green marble from a box containing 3 green and 5 blue marbles and picking the number 8 from a box with the numbers 1 to 9?

Solution: $P(\text{green}) = \frac{3}{8}$ $P(8) = \frac{1}{9}$

Therefore $P(\text{green and 8}) = \frac{3}{8} \cdot \frac{1}{9} = \frac{3}{72} = \frac{1}{24}$

Example 2: What is the probability of selecting 2 green marbles from a bag that contains 3 green and 5 blue marbles? (No replacement)

Solution: $P(\text{green}) = \frac{3}{8}$ $P(\text{2nd green}) = \frac{2}{7}$

Therefore $P(\text{2 greens}) = \frac{3}{8} \cdot \frac{2}{7} = \frac{6}{56} = \frac{3}{28}$

NOTICE THESE 2 EVENTS WERE DEPENDENT

1. If two coins are tossed, what is the probability of getting one tail and one head?

    _____

2. If the probability of winning the first game is $\frac{1}{5}$ and the probability of winning the second game is $\frac{3}{4}$, what is the probability of winning both the first and the second game?

    _____

3. Two fair dice are tossed. Each die has six faces numbered 1 to 6. What is the probability that each die shows a 2?

    _____

4. A single die is rolled twice. What is the probability of obtaining a 3 on the first roll and then a 4 on the second roll?

    _____

5. A pair of dice (1 green and 1 red) is tossed once. What is the probability of getting a 6 on the green and a 2 on the red die?

    _____

6. Assume that there is an equal probability of a baby being born on a given day of the week and that there is also an equal probability of a baby being either male or female. What is the probability that a baby will be:

    (a) female and born on Saturday? _____

    (b) male and born on a day starting with the letter T? _____

    (c) male and born on a day not starting with the letter T? _____

7. A bag contains 3 red and 6 green pens. One pen is drawn, its color noted and returned. A second pen is drawn and its color noted. What is the probability that:

    (a) both pens are red? _____

    (b) the first is red and the second is green? _____

    (c) both pens are green? _____

8. Two cubes whose faces are numbered 1 to 6 are tossed. What is the probability that both cubes show the same number?

    _____

Chapter 7
PROBABILITY AND STATISTICS

Events A or B

> **REMEMBER**
> The probability of event A, P(A) or the probability of event B, P(B), occurring is the sum of the probabilities. If there is overlap then make sure to subtract the overlapping events after adding.
>
> **Example 1:** What is the probability of picking an ace or a King?
>
> **Solution:** P(ace) = $\frac{4}{52}$ = $\frac{1}{13}$, P(King) = $\frac{4}{52}$ = $\frac{1}{13}$ Ans. $\frac{2}{13}$
>
> **Notice:** What is the probability of picking an ace or a diamond?
>
> P(ace) = $\frac{4}{52}$ = $\frac{1}{13}$, P(diamond) = $\frac{13}{52}$ = $\frac{1}{4}$, however, one ace is also a diamond so solution is $\frac{4}{52} + \frac{13}{52} - \frac{1}{52} = \frac{16}{52} = \frac{4}{13}$ Ans.

1. From a standard deck of 52 cards one card is drawn. What is the probability that it will be either a club or a diamond?

   (1) $\frac{8}{52}$ (3) $\frac{26}{52}$
   (2) $\frac{2}{52}$ (4) $\frac{12}{52}$

   _____

2. A purse contains 5 pennies, 6 dimes, and 8 quarters. If one coin is drawn at random from the purse, what is the probability that a penny or a quarter is picked?

   _____

3. From a standard deck of 52 cards, a single card is drawn at random. What is the probability that the card drawn is an ace or a red four?

   (1) $\frac{8}{52}$ (3) $\frac{6}{26}$
   (2) $\frac{6}{52}$ (4) $\frac{3}{14}$

   _____

4. A six-sided fair die is rolled. What is the probability of rolling:

   (a) a 5 or a 6?   _____

   (b) 5 or less?   _____

   (c) even number or less than 3?   _____

   (d) a 4 or less than 2?   _____

   (e) odd number or greater than 4?   _____

5. From a standard deck of cards, what is the probability of randomly picking on one draw:

   (a) a red card or a black king?   _____

   (b) a red card or a five?   _____

   (c) an ace or a club?   _____

   (d) a club or a diamond?   _____

   (e) a face card or an ace?   _____

Chapter 7
PROBABILITY AND STATISTICS

Mode, Mean and Median

REMEMBER

Example: If Charlie's grades are 80, 70, 74 and 80 find:

(1) The mode is the most often repeated value: Ans. 80

(2) The mean (average) is the sum of all the values divided by the number of values: 80 + 70 + 74 + 80 = 304 ÷ 4 = Ans. 76

(3) The median is the average of the two middle values when the values are arranged in order: 70, 74, 80, 80 are the value arranged in order and the average of the 2 middle values = (74 + 80) ÷ 2 = Ans. 77

Note: If the number of values is odd then the median is the middle value after they are arranged in order.

---

1. Given the data:
   (a) 56, 28, 32, 28, 56, 28, 49, 25, 35
   (b) 45, 80, 45, 90, 160, 60, 150
   (c) 8, 8, 10, 16, 18, 24
   (d) 60, 70, 60, 74
   (e) 70, 80, 24, 80, 60, 65, 90

   Find:
	MEAN	MODE	MEDIAN
(a)			
(b)			
(c)			
(d)			
(e)			

2. The heights of five students are given in inches as 60, 68, 72, 72 and 65. What is the median height?

3. If the mean of 65, x, 70 is 68, what is the value of x?

4. Which measure is always the same as the 50th percentile?
   (1) mean   (3) mode
   (2) median   (4) upper quartile

5. Given the set of numbers {60, 68, 73, x, 82, 88, 90}. If the median is 81, what is the value of x?

6. In the set of scores below, how many scores are less than the mean?
   61, 72, 63, 76

7. Ted recorded the number of minutes spent watching television for a week as 45, 80, 45, 90, 160, 60, 150. What is the mean number of minutes spent watching television?

Chapter 7
PROBABILITY AND STATISTICS

Quartiles and Percentiles

REMEMBER

The lower quartile (25th percentile) is the bottom 25%.
The median (50th percentile) is the middle score or interval.

---

1. On a math test 5 out of 20 students scored 80 or above. A score of 80 on this test would be the:

   (1) lower quartile   (3) upper quartile
   (2) median   (4) 80th percentile

   _____

2. On the SAT, Richard scored at the 90th percentile. Which statement is true?

   (1) Richard answered 90 questions correctly.
   (2) Ten students scored higher than Richard.
   (3) Ninety percent of the students who took the test had a score equal to or less than Richard's score.
   (4) Richard scored 90% on his SAT.

   _____

3. The histogram below shows the distribution of temperature for eleven days. Which temperature is the median?

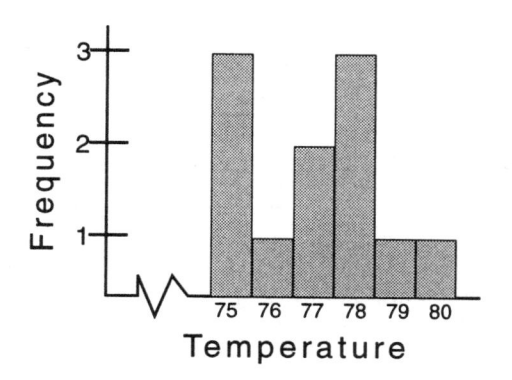

   _____

4. If the median of the grades in a Seq. 1 class is 75, which is true?

   (1) 50% of the students grades are over 75.
   (2) 75% of the students grades are over 75.
   (3) There are 75 students in the class.
   (4) 50 is the middle score.

   _____

5. The cumulative frequency table shows the distribution of scores on a math test. Which interval contains the 75th percentile?

Interval	Cumulative Frequency
61-70	4
61-80	10
61-90	14
61-100	18

   _____

6. In a basketball game 6 out of 8 team members scored under ten points in a game. If Ted scored over 10 points he would fall in the:

   (1) lower 10th percentile   (3) median
   (2) lower quartile   (4) upper quartile

   _____

7. A census taker visited 100 homes. The accompanying table shows the frequencies for the number of people living in each home. Which interval contains the median for these data?

Interval	Frequency
1-2	40
3-4	39
5-6	16
7-8	5

   _____

89

Chapter 7
PROBABILITY AND STATISTICS

Mixed Problems

> **REMEMBER**
> To find a missing score if the average is known, write an equation representing the missing score by x.
>
> **Example:** A student receives test scores of 81, 95, 92 and 88. What must the fifth score be so that the mean will be exactly 91?
>
> **Solution:** If x is the missing score then $\frac{81+95+92+88+x}{5} = 91$
>
> $\frac{356+x}{5} = 91$ or $356 + x = 455$: therefore $x = 99$

1. Dan bowled 3 games with scores of 140, 130 and 170. If he wants to maintain his average which is 150, what must his score be in the fourth game?

2. For the group of data, 10, 10, 15, 18, 32, which is true?
   (1) mode > mean (3) mode > median
   (2) mean > median (4) mean = median

3. For the set of data, 2, 6, 8, 8, which statement is true?
   (1) mean > mode (3) median < mode
   (2) mean > median (4) mode = median

4. Express in terms of x, the mean of (3x - 9) and (5x + 3).

5. Ann took seven tests and got different grades on each test. If one of the grades is selected at random, what is the probability that the grade will be greater than the median?

6. For the data, 20, 30, 40, 40, 80, 90, which statement is true?
   (1) mean < mode   (3) mode = mean
   (2) mode = median (4) median < mode

7. What is the average (mean) of (2x + 1), (3x - 5) and (x + 10)?

8. If the average of 60, 75, 75, 80, x is 76, find x.

9. For which set of data do the mean, median and mode all have the same value?
   (1) 2,2,2,5,8   (3) 2,4,5,6,2
   (2) 2,2,4,4,4   (4) 2,5,5,5,8

10. If the average (mean) for following data is 10, what is the fifth score?
    6, 9, 12, 4, ?

90

Chapter 7
PROBABILITY AND STATISTICS
Chapter Test

1. What is the mode for the following data?
   5, 6, 6, 7, 9, 10, 11

   _____

2. Evaluate $_7P_5$.

   _____

3. Rosa wants to attend college at one of three colleges and major in one of four areas. In how many different ways can Rosa make her plans?

   _____

4. A team consists of 25 girls. The table below shows the points each player scored. Which interval contains the median?

Interval	Frequency
101-125	3
76-100	6
51-75	9
26-50	5
0-25	2

   _____

5. If the probability that Jane will NOT be elected class president is $\frac{12}{17}$, what is the probability that she will be elected class president?

   _____

6. From a standard deck of 52 cards, one card is drawn. What is the probability that it will be a queen?

   (1) $\frac{1}{52}$ (3) $\frac{13}{52}$
   (2) $\frac{4}{52}$ (4) $\frac{2}{52}$

   _____

7. For the set of data 9, 11, 11, 14, and 20, which statement is true?

   (1) mean = mode
   (2) mean < mode
   (3) median > mode
   (4) mean > median

   _____

8. How many different signals can be sent if 4 different flags are arranged in different order for each signal?

   _____

9. Evaluate: $\frac{8!}{5!}$

   _____

10. On a game show, the "dragon" is hidden behind one of nine panels. What is the probability of selecting the panel with the dragon?

    (1) 1   (3) $\frac{1}{9}$
    (2) $\frac{8}{9}$ (4) 8

    _____

11. A single six-sided die is rolled. What is the probability of rolling a 2?

    _____

12. Express in terms of x the mean of (5x + 3) and (7x + 9).

    _____

13. What is the mean of the following scores:
    50, 50, 52, 56

    (1) 50   (3) 52
    (2) 51   (4) 208

    _____

Chapter 7
PROBABILITY AND STATISTICS
Chapter Test (Continued)

14. If a pair of dice is tossed, what is the probability that the sum is even?

15. If 2 coins are tossed simultaneously, how many outcomes are possible?

16. What is the probability of scoring 100% or less on a mathematics test?

17. A contest offers a prize of a trip to Paris, Rome or Athens in spring, summer or fall. How many different choices are possible if a prize consists of one city and one season?

18. The histogram below shows the distribution of salaries for 575 families. Which salary is the mode?

19. Melissa has received grades of 80, 85, 90, and 98 for the first 4 quarters. If she wants to get an average of 90 for the year, what should she get on her final exam?

20. The probability of an event occurring is represented by P(E). If $P(E) = \frac{2}{11}$, then the probability that the event will NOT occur is:

    (1) 1   (3) 0

    (2) $\frac{9}{11}$ (4) $\frac{11}{2}$

21. If a number is picked at random from the set {-5, -4, -3, -2, -1, 0, 1, 2, 3, 4, 5}, what is the probability that the number satisfies the equation $x^2 - 25 = 0$?

22. In how many different ways can 4 students be seated in 4 seats?

23. From a standard deck of cards, what is the probability of picking on one draw, a ten or an ace?

24. If the average of 4, 6, 6, 8, 10, 14, x, 24 is 12, find the value of x.

25. A pair of dice (1 green and 1 red) is tossed once. What is the probability of getting a 5 on the green die and a 1 on the red die?

Chapter 8
TRANSFORMATIONS

Line Reflections

> **REMEMBER**
>
> A line reflection is the image that is mirrored over a line. The notation r_n (EF) means EF is reflected in line n.
>
> **Example:** The reflections at **pop** over line m would be **bob** 
>
> A point reflection is the image that is equidistant on the other side of a point.
>
> **Example:** The reflection of AB through point P would result in A'B'

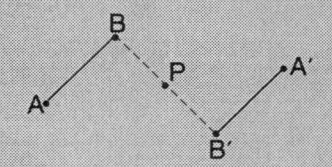

1. If the point (-6,2) is reflected over the y-axis, the coordinates of the image point are:

   (1) (2,-6)   (3) (-6,-2)
   (2) (-2,6)   (4) (6,2)

2. In the accompanying diagram, which triangle is the image of △3 after a reflection in the y-axis:

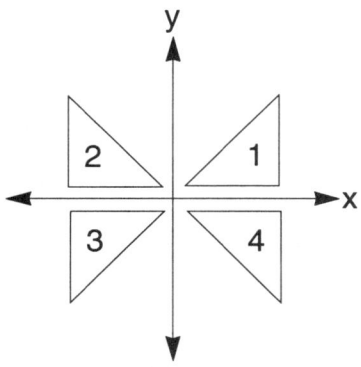

   (1) 1   (3) 3
   (2) 2   (4) 4

3. If the point (2,4) is reflected over the x-axis, what are the coordinates of the image point?

4. In the accompanying figure, what point is the image of r_m(C)?

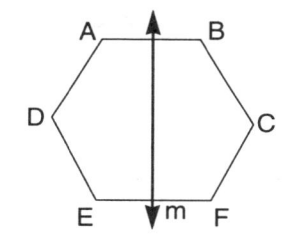

5. When point A (-3,5) is reflected over the line x = 1, the image is:

   (1) (5,-3)   (3) (4,5)
   (2) (3,5)   (4) (5,5)

6. Name the image of point F under line reflection r_n.

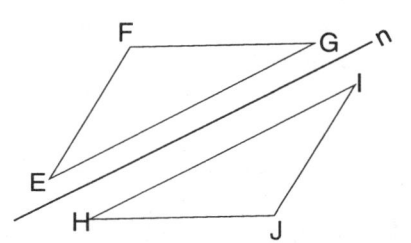

93

Chapter 8
TRANSFORMATIONS

Translations

REMEMBER

A translation can be considered as a "slide" of a figure. The notation $T_{2,5}$ means that if (3,2) is translated (or slid) 2 units right and 5 units up the result will be 3 + 2 for the x-coordinate and 2 + 5 for the y-coordinate or (5,7).

Example: If △ABC is translated 6 units right and 1 unit up the result (image) will be A'B'C'.

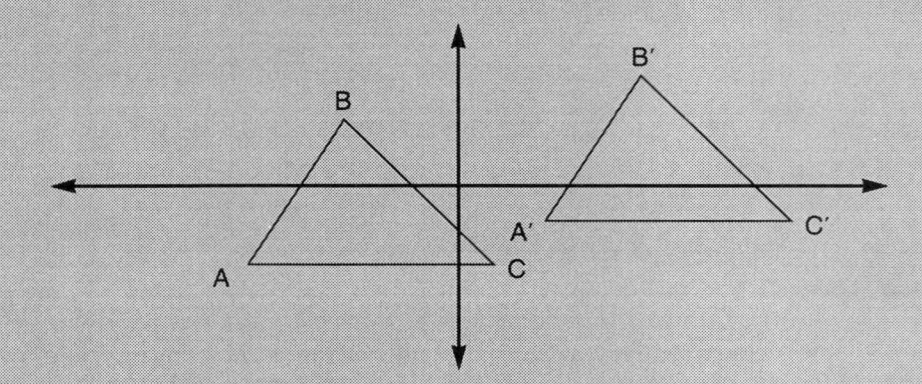

1. Find the coordinates of the image of the point (2,-3) under $T_{3,1}$.

2. Which translation maps (4,2) → (8,6)?
    (1) $T_{12,8}$ (3) $T_{4,8}$
    (2) $T_{4,4}$ (4) $T_{12,4}$

3. Find the coordinates of the image of the point (-4,7) under $T_{-3,-4}$.

4. If a translation $T_{1,-2}$ maps (x,5) onto (8,3), what is the value of x?

5. If a translation $T_{-3,6}$ maps (4,y) onto (1,5), what is the value of y?

6. In the diagram below, a translation maps C onto J. Name the images for each of the following points under the same translation.

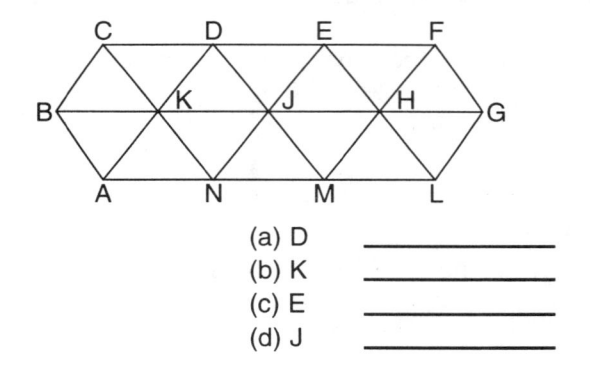

    (a) D _____
    (b) K _____
    (c) E _____
    (d) J _____

7. △A'B'C' is the image of △ABC below. Which type of transformation is represented by △A'B'C'?

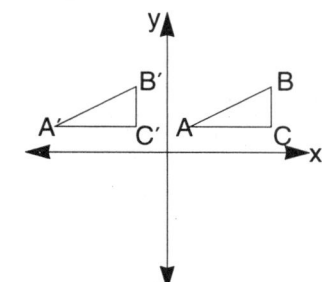

94

Chapter 8
TRANSFORMATIONS

Rotations

REMEMBER

A rotation can be thought of as turning a figure about some fixed point. The notation $R_{P,180°}$ means rotating a figure about point P an angle of 180° (counterclockwise).

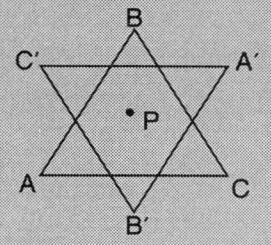

If equilateral triangle ABC is rotated 180° about point P the result (image) will be equilateral triangle A'B'C'. This is also called a half-turn.

---

1. Figure B is the image of figure A under which transformation?

   (1) line reflection
   (2) rotation
   (3) translation
   (4) dilation _____

2. In the accompanying diagram, a square is inscribed in circle O. Find the result of each of the following rotations.

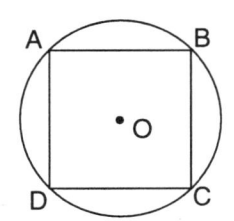

   (a) $R_{O,90°}$ (A) _____
   (b) $R_{O,180°}$ (D) _____
   (c) $R_{O,360°}$ (B) _____
   (d) $R_{O,270°}$ (C) _____
   (e) $R_{O,-90°}$ (B) _____

3. If T is rotated 90°, the image is:

   (1) ⊣   (3) ⊥
   (2) ⊢   (4) T _____

4. If K is rotated 180°, which is the resulting figure?

   (1) ⋊   (3) ⋈
   (2) ⊼   (4) K _____

5. For each of the following letters draw the resulting figure under the rotation given.

   (a) L, $R_{90°}$ _____
   (b) A, $R_{180°}$ _____
   (c) H, $R_{-90°}$ _____
   (d) U, $R_{270°}$ _____
   (e) Y, $R_{180°}$ _____

6. Which diagram below represents the image of △ 2 when rotated 90° clockwise about the origin?

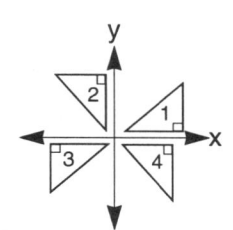

   (1) 1   (3) 3
   (2) 2   (4) 4 _____

Chapter 8
TRANSFORMATIONS

Dilations

REMEMBER
A dilation can be thought of as reducing or enlarging a figure. The notation D_2 means to enlarge a figure or a point to twice its original size.

Example: Find the image of (3,-5) under the dilation D_3. The answer is (9,-15) because the point (3,-5) should be multiplied by 3.

1. Which of the following transformations is a dilation?
   (1) (2,5) → (3,6)
   (2) (2,5) → (5,2)
   (3) (2,5) → (-2,5)
   (4) (2,5) → (4,10)

   _____

2. Which of the following transformations maps (3,-1) → (-6,2)?
   (1) T_{-6} (3) D_{-2}
   (2) D_2 (4) D_{-3}

   _____

3. Find the image of each of the following points under the dilation D_5.
   (a) (6,2) _____
   (b) (-3,6) _____
   (c) (0,1) _____
   (d) (8,-6) _____
   (e) (-1,0) _____

4. Under a certain transformation △A'B'C' is the image of △ABC. The perimeter of △A'B'C' is three time the perimeter of △ABC. The transformation is:
   (1) $D_{\frac{1}{3}}$ (3) $D_{-\frac{1}{3}}$
   (2) D_{-3} (4) D_3

   _____

5. If the coordinates of triangle ABC are A(1,2), B(2,5) and C(4,8), what are the coordinates of its image A'B'C' after D_2?

   A' = _____
   B' = _____
   C' = _____

6. Find the dilation for each of the following transformations.
   (a) (5,2) → (10,4) _____
   (b) (-1,3) → (-3,9) _____
   (c) (4,-2) → (2,-1) _____
   (d) (-2,6) → (2,-6) _____
   (e) (7,1) → (-14,-2) _____

7. Which of the following transformations maps (2,3) → (-2,-3)?
   (1) T_{-1} (3) $T_{1,1}$
   (2) D_{-1} (4) D_0

   _____

8. If the image of (2,-1) under dilation D_4 is (x,-4), find the value of x.

   _____

Chapter 8
TRANSFORMATIONS

Line and Point Symmetry

REMEMBER

A figure has point symmetry if the figure coincides with itself when it is rotated 180° in either direction.

A figure has line symmetry if at least one line can be drawn through the figure so that half of it is mirrored.

Examples:

Isosceles triangle ABC has vertical line symmetry because the right side is the reflection of the left side when a vertical line is drawn.

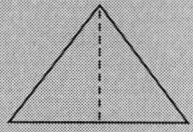

The letter S has point symmetry because it coincides with itself when it is rotated 180°

1. Which figure always has exactly one line of symmetry?

    (1) isosceles trapezoid

    (2) parallelogram

    (3) hexagon

    (4) rectangle

    _____

2. The capital letter "M" has:

    (1) line symmetry, only

    (2) point symmetry, only

    (3) both point and line symmetry

    (4) neither point nor line symmetry

    _____

3. Circle each of the letters that have only point symmetry.

    | D | S |
    | E | T |
    | H | U |
    | I | V |
    | O | X |
    | P | Z |

4. Which letters have both point and line symmetry.

    | A | I |
    | B | T |
    | C | V |
    | H | X |

    _____

5. State whether each figure has point symmetry and/or line symmetry.

    (a) square

    (b) rectangle

    (c) parallelogram

    (d) rhombus

    (e) trapezoid

    (f) hexagon

    (g) circle

    (h) triangle

    (i) trapezoid

    (j) pentagon

    _____   _____
    Point Symmetry   Line Symmetry

97

Chapter 8
TRANSFORMATIONS
Chapter Test

1. If the point (6,-4) is reflected over the y-axis, what are the coordinates of the image point?

   _____

2. If R is rotated 90°, the resulting figure is:

   (1) ᴙ   (3) ᖴ
   (2) ᴚ   (4) R

   _____

3. Find the coordinates of the image of (-7,5) under $T_{2,1}$

   _____

4. Which transformation is illustrated in the diagram?

   (1) a reflection   (3) a rotation
   (2) a dilation   (4) a translation

   _____

5. Which of the following transformations maps A onto B in the diagram?

   (1) $R_{O,90}$ (3) $r_m(A)$
   (2) $R_n(A)$ (4) $R_{O,180}$

   _____

6. Show the reflection of $\overline{CD}$ in line m and label it AB.

   _____

7. If a translation $T_{4,5}$ maps (3,1) onto (x,6), what is the value of x?

   (1) 1   (3) -3
   (2) 7   (4) 8

   _____

8. In the accompanying figure, which point is the image of $R_{180}(X)$?

   (1) W   (3) R
   (2) Y   (4) S

   _____

9. If the image of D_3 is (3,6), then which of the following is the pre-image?

   (1) (0,3)   (3) (6,9)
   (2) (1,2)   (4) (9,18)

   _____

10. Which letter has line symmetry only?

    (1) X   (3) Z
    (2) T   (4) S

    _____

11. If the point (3,-11) is reflected over the x-axis, the image is:

    (1) (3,11)   (3) (-3,-11)
    (2) (-11,3)   (4) (11,-3)

    _____

SEQUENTIAL MATHEMATICS COURSE 1

REGENTS REVIEW

PART II

TAUTOLOGIES

Example: In a truth table, if every element in the last column is true, then the last column is a tautology.

In solving the following tautology, the following truth table will be helpful to you:

p	[negation] ~p	q	"or" [disjunction] p ∨ q	"and" [conjunction] p ∧ q	"if...then" [conditional] p → q	"if and only if" [biconditional] p ↔ q
T	F	T	T	T	T	T
T	F	F	T	F	F	F
F	T	T	T	F	T	F
F	T	F	F	F	T	T

1a. Complete the truth table for the statement:
[p ∨ (~p ∧ q)] ↔ (p ∨ q)

p	q	~p	~p ∧ q	p ∨ (~p ∧ q)	p ∨ q	[p ∨ (~p ∧ q)] ↔ (p ∨ q)
T	T					
T	F					
F	T					
F	F					

1b. Using the results from part a, is [p ∨ (~p ∧ q)] ↔ (p ∨ q) a tautology?

ANSWER
1a.

p	q	~p	~p ∧ q	p ∨ (~p ∧ q)	p ∨ q	[p ∨ (~p ∧ q)] ↔ (p ∨ q)
T	T	F	F	T	T	T
T	F	F	F	T	T	T
F	T	T	T	T	T	T
F	F	T	F	F	F	T

1b. It is a tautology because it is true regardless of the truth values assigned to the simple sentences in the first two columns. (Every element in the last column is true.)

PRACTICE PROBLEMS

1a. Finish the following chart: [8]
b. Using the results from a., is the statement in the last column a tautology? [2]

p	q	~q	p ∧ q	p → ~q	~(p → ~q)	~(p → ~q) ↔ (p ∧ q)
T	T			F		
T	F	T				
F	T				F	T
F	F		F			

100

TAUTOLOGIES
(Continued)

2 a. Complete the following chart : [8]
  b. Using the results from a., is the statement in the last column a tautology and why? [2]

p	q	~q	p∧q	p ∨ (p∧q)	[p∨ (p∧q)] →~q
T	T				
T	F				
F	T				
F	F				

3a. Complete the following truth table: [8]
  b. Using the results from a, is the statement ~(p → ~q) ↔ (p ∧ q) a tautology? [2]

p	q	~q	p∧q	p → ~q	~(p → ~q)	~(p → ~q) ↔ (p∧q)
T	T					
T	F					
F	T					
F	F					

4a. Construct a truth table for the statement:
   ~(p → q) ↔ (p ∧ ~q)   [8]
  b. Using the results from a., is the statement a tautology? [2]

5. Each part below consists of three statements. The truth values for two statements in each set are given. Based on this information, determine the truth value of the remaining statement. Next to each letter, write the missing truth value (TRUE or FALSE). If the truth value cannot be determined from the information given, write "CANNOT BE DETERMINED".

	STATEMENTS	TRUTH VALUE		STATEMENTS	TRUTH VALUE
a)(1)	p ∧ ~q	TRUE	c)(1)	p ↔ q	TRUE
(2)	p	TRUE	(2)	p	FALSE
(3)	q	_____ [2]	(3)	~q	_____ [2]
b)(1)	p	TRUE	d)(1)	~p ∨ ~q	FALSE
(2)	q	FALSE	(2)	p	_____ [2]
(3)	p → ~q	_____ [2]	(3)	q	TRUE

TAUTOLOGIES
(Continued)

6a. Write the converse, inverse and contrapositive for:
"If I receive a loan, then I will buy an automobile." [8]

b. What is logically equivalent to the conditional in a.? [2]

7a. Construct a truth table for the statement:
$[(p \to q) \land \sim p] \to \sim q$ [8]

b. Using the results from a., is the statement a tautology and why? [2]

8a. Construct a truth table for the statement:
$\sim(p \lor q) \to (\sim p \land \sim q)$ [8]

b. Using the results from a., is the statement a tautology? [2]

9. Each part consists of a set of three statements. For the third statement write the truth value (TRUE or FALSE). If the truth value cannot be determined from the information given, write "CANNOT BE DETERMINED".

(1) Paul is smart or Ann is not pretty.   T
    Ann is pretty.   T
    Paul is smart.   _____ [2]

(2) If it is May, then it is spring.   T
    It is not spring.   F
    It is not May.   _____ [2]

(3) It is raining and it is warm.   F
    It is raining.   F
    It is warm.   _____ [2]

PYTHAGOREAN THEOREM

In solving for the missing side of a right triangle, the Pythagorean Theorem $a^2 + b^2 = c^2$ will be used.

Example: The legs of a right triangle are represented by x and x - 2. The hypotenuse is 10.

a) Find x   [3,5]
b) Find the area of the triangle   [2]

Solution:

a) To find x, use $a^2 + b^2 = c^2$ and substitute x for a, (x-2) for b and 10 for c as follows:
$x^2 + (x-2)^2 = 10^2$

Now simplify and solve the equation:

$x^2 + x^2 - 4x + 4 = 100$	multiply (x-2)(x-2)
$2x^2 - 4x - 96 = 0$	subtract 100
$x^2 - 2x - 48 = 0$	divide by 2
(x-8)(x+6) = 0	factor
x-8 = 0 x+6 = 0	set each factor = 0
x = 8 x = -6	
and x - 2 = 8 - 2 = 6 reject x = -6	

b) To find the area use the formula $A = \frac{1}{2}bh$ where b = 8, h = 6 therefore $A = \frac{1}{2}(8)(6) = 24$

---

1. The length of the hypotenuse of a right triangle is 10. The length of the longer leg exceeds the length of the shorter leg by 2. Find the length of the shorter leg. [Only an algebraic solution will be accepted.} [5,5]

---

2. The hypotenuse of a right triangle is represented by 3x + 4 and one leg is represented by x. The other leg is 24.

   (a) Find x   [3,3]
   (b) Find the hypotenuse   [2]
   (c) Find the area of the triangle   [2]

PYTHAGOREAN THEOREM
(Continued)

3. The length of the hypotenuse of a right triangle is 13. The length of the shorter leg is seven less than the length of the longer leg. Find the length of the longer leg. [Only an algebraic solution will be accepted.] [5,5]

4. The length of the hypotenuse of a right triangle is 15. If the longer leg is three more than the shorter leg, find the length of the shorter leg. [Only an algebraic solution will be accepted.] [5,5]

5. The hypotenuse of a right triangle is 5 and the legs are represents by x and x + 1.

    (a) Find x   [3,3]
    (b) Find the perimeter of the triangle   [2]
    (c) Find the area of the triangle   [2]

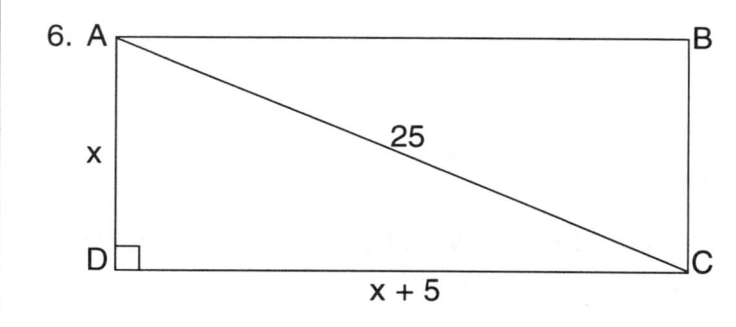

6. In rectangle ABCD, two adjacent sides are represented by x and x + 5. If diagonal AC = 25, find

    (a) the value of x   [7]
    (b) the area of rectangle ABCD   [3]

NUMBER PROBLEMS

Example: One positive number is 5 more than another. The sum of their squares is 193. Find the numbers. [Only an algebraic solution will be accepted]. [5,5]

Solution: Let x = the positive number and x + 5 represent the other number.

The squares of the numbers would then be x^2 and (x + 5)(x + 5).

Since the sum of their squares is 193,

x^2 + (x + 5)(x + 5) = 193

$x^2 + x^2$ + 5x + 5x + 25 = 193

$2x^2$ + 10x + 25 = 193

$2x^2$ + 10x + 25 - 193 = 0

$2x^2$ + 10x - 168 = 0

Now divide all terms by 2 to simplify
x^2 + 5x - 84 = 0

Factor: (x + 12)(x - 7) = 0

x + 12 = 0   x - 7 = 0
x = -12   x = 7

disregard -12   x + 5 = 12 ANS (7,12)

check: Sum of squares is 193

(7)(7) + (12)(12) = 193
49   +   144   = 193
193   = 193 check

---

1. One number is 6 more than another number. If four times the smaller number is decreased by twice the larger number, the result is 4. Find both numbers. [5,5]

2. The square of a positive number is 56 more than the number itself. What is the number? [Only an algebraic solution will be accepted.] [5,5]

3. One positive number is three less than another positive number. If the square of the sum of the two numbers is 49, find both numbers. [5,5]

NUMBER PROBLEMS
(Continued)

4. One number is 9 more than another number. If the product of the two numbers is -20, find both numbers. [5,5]

5. One positive number is 8 more than another. The sum of their squares is 104. Find both numbers. [5,5]

6. The square of a positive number is 21 more than 4 times the number. Find the number. [5,5]

7. The square of a positive number decreased by 2 times the number is 24. Find the positive number. [5,5]

(Continued)

NUMBER PROBLEMS

8a. The ratio of two numbers is 7:2. The two numbers add up to 90. Find the two numbers. [5]

b. The ratio of two numbers is 8:1. If the larger number exceeds the smaller number by 21, find both numbers. [5]

9a. In triangle XYZ, the measure of angle Y is 40 more than the measure of angle X. The measure of angle Z is 10 less than three times angle X. Find the measure of angle X. [5]

b. Five more than three times x is greater than 31. Find the smallest integer for x. [5]

10a. In triangle ABC, the measure of angle B is twice as large as the measure of angle A. The measure of angle C is 20 more than the measure of angle A. Find the measure of angle A. [5]

b. Six more than eight times x is less than 48. Find the largest integer for x. [5]

11. Three numbers are in the ratio of 4:7:9. If the larger number is multiplied by 4, the result is 50 more than the sum of the first and second numbers. Find the three numbers. [5,5]

CONSECUTIVE INTEGER PROBLEMS

Example: Find three consecutive positive odd integers such that the product of the two smaller exceeds the largest by 26. [5,5]

Solution: Let x = 1st positive odd integer
x + 2 = 2nd positive odd integer
and x + 4 = 3rd positive odd integer

Remember: If the word EVEN or ODD is used, we use x, x +2, and x + 4. If the word even or odd is NOT USED, we use x, x + 1, and x + 2 for consecutive integers.

The product of the two smaller exceeds the larger by 26.

$x(x+2) = x + 4 + 26$

$x^2 + 2x = x + 30$

$x^2 + 2x - x - 30 = 0$

$x^2 + x - 30 = 0$

$(x + 6)(x - 5) = 0$

x + 6 = 0   x - 5 = 0
x = -6   x = 5
disregard -6   x + 2 = 7
               x + 4 = 9   Ans. (5,7,9)

check:
The product of the two smaller exceeds the larger by 26.
(5)(7) = 9 + 26
35 = 35 check

---

1. Find three consecutive odd integers such that the product of the two smaller exceeds the largest by 52. [5,5]

2. Find three consecutive even integers such that the product of the two smaller exceeds the largest by 38. [5,5]

3. Find three consecutive integers such that the square of the first exceeds the sum of the second and third by 45. [5,5]

4. The sum of the squares of two positive consecutive odd integers is 130. What are the integers? [5,5]

CONSECUTIVE INTEGER PROBLEMS

(Continued)

5. Two positive numbers are consecutive odd integers. The square of the smaller is 10 less than 5 times the larger. Find the integers. [5,5]

8. The length of one leg of a right triangle is 5. The lengths of the other leg and the hypotenuse are consecutive integers. Find the length of the hypotenuse. [6,4]

[Hint: Leg² + Leg² = Hypotenuse²]

6. Find the smallest of three consecutive positive integers such that the product of the two smaller integers is 68 more than twice the largest integer. [5,5]

9. The length of one leg of a right triangle is 6. The lengths of the other leg and the hypotenuse are consecutive even integers. Find the length of the hypotenuse. [6,4]

7. Find three consecutive positive odd integers such that the square of the smallest exceeds twice the largest by 91. [5,5]

10. The sum of the squares of two consecutive positive even integers is 164. Find the integers. [4,6]

VERBAL INEQUALITY PROBLEMS

Example: The length of a rectangle is 5 cm less than 2 times its width. What are the dimensions if the perimeter will be at least 32 cm?

Solution:

1) Represent the variables
   Let x be the width, 2x - 5 be the length

2) Write the inequality
   Hint: For "AT LEAST" or "SMALLEST POSSIBLE" use "$\geq$".
   For "AT MOST" or "GREATEST POSSIBLE" use "$\leq$".
   so: $2x + 2(2x - 5) \geq 32$
   twice width + twice length is at least 32

3) Solve the inequality
   $2x + 4x - 10 \geq 32$ Substitute 7 in 2x - 5 to find length
   $6x - 10 \geq 32$
   $6x \geq 42$
   $x \geq 7$ $2(7) - 5 = 9$
                              therefore
                              $2x - 5 \geq 9$

   The width must be ≥ 7 and the length must be ≥ 9.

---

1. The larger of two integers is 7 times the smaller. If the sum of the two integers is greater than 40, find the smallest possible value of x. [Only an algebraic solution will be accepted.]   [5,5]

2. Paul wants to design a rectangular room so that its length is 3 meters more than its width, and its perimeter is less than 19 meters. If each of the dimensions of the room must be a whole number of meters, what are the greatest possible measures in meters of the length and the width? [Only an algebraic solution will be accepted.]   [5,5]

VERBAL INEQUALITY PROBLEMS
(Continued)

3a. Five less than twice x is greater than 31. Find the smallest integer for x. [Only an algebraic solution will be accepted.] [5]

b. One more than three times x is less than 16. Find the greatest integer for x. [Only an algebraic solution will be accepted.] [5]

4. The sum of two consecutive even integers is at most 30. What are the greatest possible integers? [Only an algebraic solution will be accepted.] [5,5]

5. The width of a rectangular room is four less than the length and its perimeter is greater than 28. What are the least possible measures of the length and the width? [Only an algebraic solution will be accepted.] [5,5]

6. The smaller of two integers is 8 less than the larger. If the sum of the two integers is less than 14, find the greatest possible value of the larger number. [Only an algebraic solution will be accepted.] [5,5]

GRAPHING SYSTEMS OF LINEAR EQUATIONS IN TWO VARIABLES

Example:

Solve the following system of equations graphically and check:

$y + x = 5$ $\qquad$ $2y = 3x$ $\qquad$ [8,2]

Solution:

1) Rewrite equations solving for y in terms of x.

$y + x = 5 \qquad 2y = 3x$

$y = -x + 5 \qquad y = \frac{3}{2}x$

2) Select values of x and find y.

x	-x + 5	y
0	0 + 5	5
1	-1 + 5	4
2	-2 + 5	3
3	-3 + 5	2

x	$\frac{3}{2}$x	y
0	$\frac{3}{2}$(0)	0
2	$\frac{3}{2}$(2)	3
4	$\frac{3}{2}$(4)	6

3) Graph the two lines.

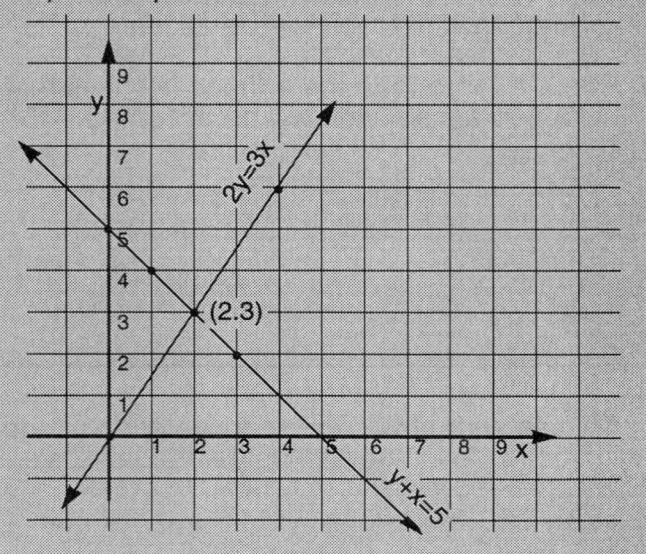

4) Read the point of intersection. (2,3)

5) Check using x = 2 and y = 3

$y + x = 5 \qquad 2y = 3x$

$3 + 2 = 5 \qquad 2(3) = 3(2)$

$5 = 5 \qquad 6 = 6$

---

1. On the same set of coordinate axes, graph the following system of equations and label the solution set.

    $y = 2x + 4$ $\qquad$ [8,2]

    $x + y = 7$

2. Solve graphically and check. [8,2]

    $y = \frac{3}{2}x$

    $y - x - 1 = 0$

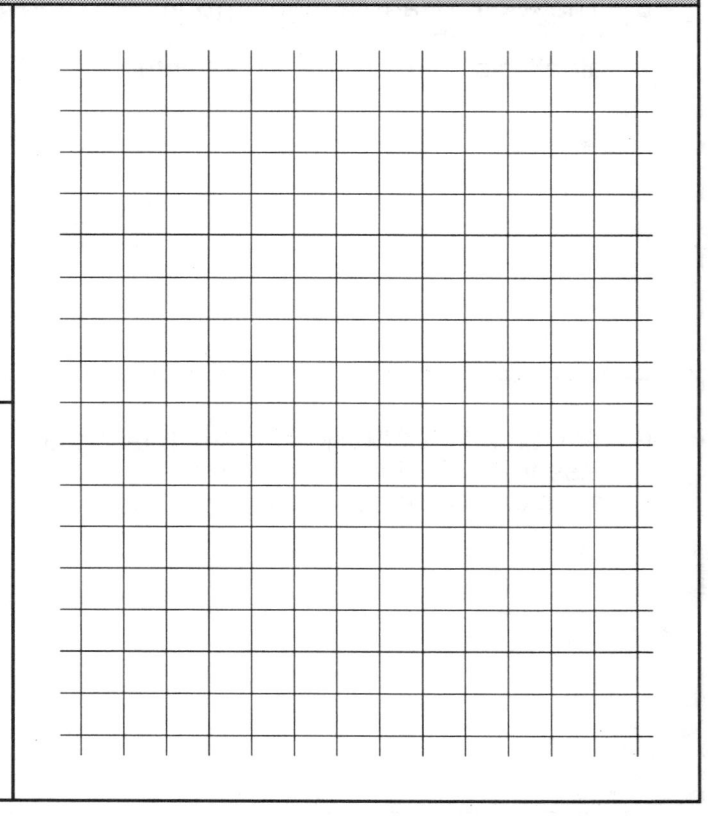

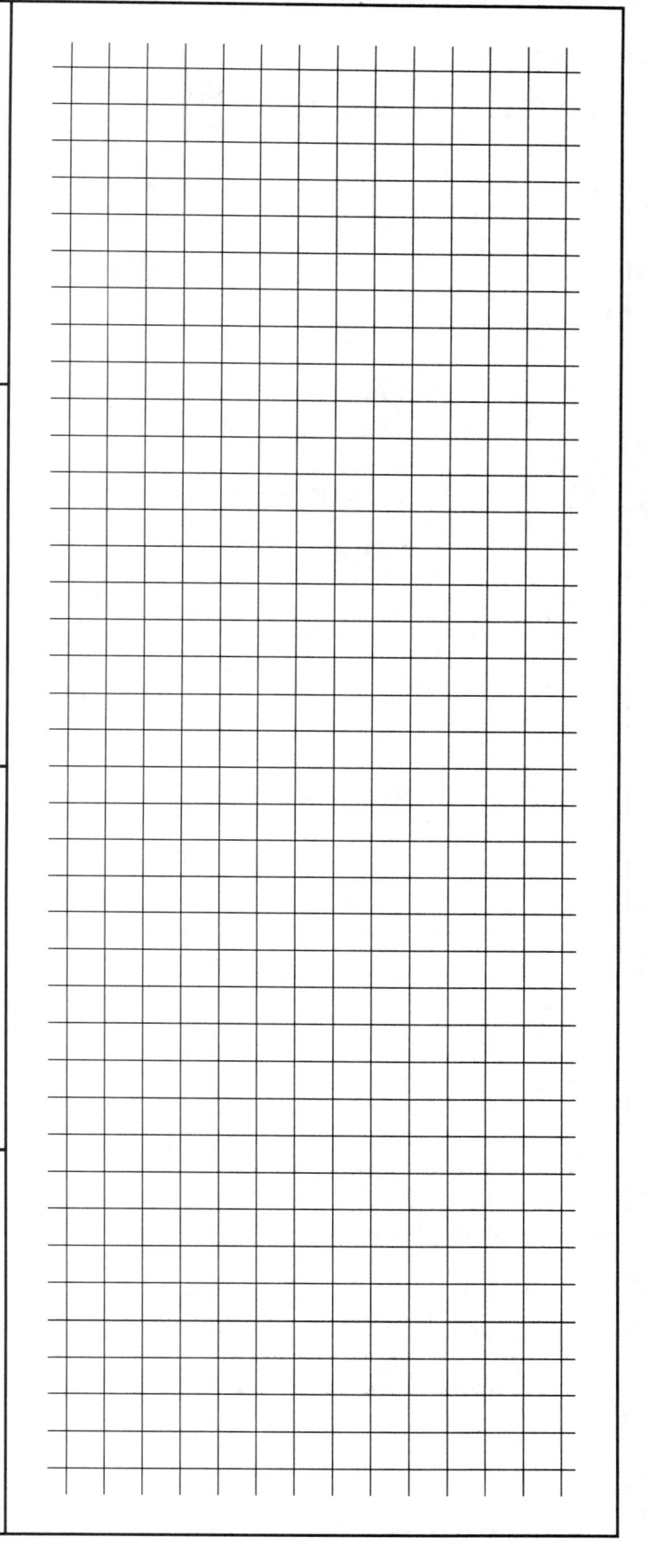

GRAPHING SYSTEMS OF LINEAR EQUATIONS IN TWO VARIABLES

(Continued)

3a. On the same set of coordinate axis, graph the following lines.

$y = 4$ [2]

$y = -2x - 2$ [3]

$3x - y = 2$ [3]

b. Find the area of the triangle formed by the intersection of the lines drawn in part a.   [2]

4. Solve the following system of equations graphically and label the solution set.

$y = \frac{3}{2}x - \frac{5}{2}$ [8,2]

$y = -\frac{4}{3}x + 6$

5. Solve graphically and check:

$y = 2x + 1$ $x + y = 4$ [8,2]

6. Solve the following system of equations graphically and check:

$x + y = -2$ $2x - y = -4$ [8,2]

ALGEBRAIC SOLUTION OF A SYSTEM OF LINEAR EQUATIONS

Example: Solve algebraically for x and y and check: $3x - y = 1$ and $x + y = 3$ [8,2]

Solution: (SUBSTITUTION METHOD)

$3x - y = 1$ $x + y = 3$
$3x = 1 + y$
$3x - 1 = y$
$y = 3x - 1$ $x + (3x - 1) = 3$
                       $x + 3x - 1 = 3$
                       $4x - 1 = 3$
                       $4x = 4$
                       $x = 1$

$y = 3(1) - 1$
$y = 3 - 1$
$y = 2$ Ans (1,2)

check:
$3x - y = 1$ $x + y = 3$
$3(1) - 2 = 1$ $1 + 2 = 3$
$3 - 2 = 1$ $3 = 3$ check
$1 = 1$ check

Solution: (ADDITION/SUBTRACTION METHOD)

$3x - y = 1$ $x + y = 3$

$3x - y = 1$
$\underline{x + y = 3}$
add like terms, $4x = 4$

divide by 4, $x = 1$

now find y, $x + y = 3$
                  $1 + y = 3$
                  $y = 3 - 1$
                  $y = 2$

check answer (1,2) same as in substitution method

---

1. Solve algebraically for x and y and check:

   $6y - 2x = 6$

   $3y - 4x = -6$ [8,2]

---

2. Solve for x and y and check:

   $2x - 2y = -6$

   $y = -2x$ [8,2]

---

3. Solve algebraically for a and b and check:

   $3a + 5b = 4$

   $4a + 3b = -2$ [8,2]

(Continued)

ALGEBRAIC SOLUTION OF A SYSTEM OF LINEAR EQUATIONS

4. Solve algebraically and check:

   $5x - 3y = -4$

   $3x + 2y = 9$ [8,2]

5. Solve the following system of equations algebraically and check:

   $y = -x + 2$

   $5x - 2y = 3$ [8,2]

6. Solve for x and y algebraically and check:

   $3x + 2y = 5$

   $2x - 3y = 12$ [8,2]

7. Solve algebraically and check:

   $3c - 3d = -12$

   $c + 2d = 2$ [8,2]

PROBLEM SOLVING

Example: A towing service charges $50.00 for a towing service call plus $1.50 per mile.

  a. A tow that costs $78.50 is for how many more miles than a tow that costs $66.50? [6]

  b. If x represents the number of miles an auto is towed and y represents the total cost of the tow, which formula could be used to find y? [2]

   (1) y = 1.50x   (3) y = 1.50 + 50.00 x
   (2) y = 50.00 + 1.50x   (4) y = 50.00 + 1.50(x-1)

  c. Using your answer from part *b*, find the value of y if x = 9. [2]

Solution:

  a. Since both tows each pay $50.00 for a service call, the cost difference must be in the mileage. The difference in cost, $78.50 - $66.50 = $12.00 for the extra mileage. Since the cost per mile is $1.50, divide the cost, $12.00 by the cost per mile, $1.50. 12 divided by 1.50 = 8 mile difference. Answer 8 miles

  b. y = 50.00 + 1.50x   answer (2)

  c. y = 50.00 + 1.50(9) = 50.00 + 13.50 = $63.50 answer

---

1. A taxi ride costs $2.75 for the first quarter of a mile and $0.85 for each subsequent quarter mile.

   a. A ride that costs $23.15 is how many miles longer than a ride that costs $17.20? [Show or explain the procedure used to obtain your answer.] [6]

   b. If x represents the number of quarter miles traveled and y represents the total cost of the trip, which formula could be used to find y? [2]

   (1) y = 2.75x   (3) y = 2.75 + 0.85(x-1)
   (2) y = 2.75 + 0.85x   (4) y = 2.75x + 0.85x

   c. Using your answer from part *b*, find the value of y if x = 15 [2]

PROBLEM SOLVING
(Continued)

2. Christopher has cut three pieces of string to attach to three kites. Two pieces are of equal length. The third piece is one-half of the length of each of the others. He cut the three pieces from a roll of string 70 meters long without any string left over. Find the number of meters in each piece. [Show or explain the procedure used to obtain your answer.] [10]

3. Allison has a square flower garden and Lauren has a rectangular flower garden. The width of the rectangular garden is 2 yards less than a side of the square garden, and the length of the rectangular garden is 5 yards more than a side of the square garden. If the sum of the areas of both Allison's and Lauren's gardens is 220 square yards, find the measure of a side of the square garden. [Show or explain the procedure used to obtain your answer.] [10]

4. For college orientation week, Mike sold 200 shirts. Sweatshirts were priced at $50.00 each and T-shirts at $20.00 each. Mike received a total of $6250.00 for the shirts. How many of each type of shirt did Mike sell for college orientation week? [Show or explain the procedure used to obtain your answer.] [10]

5. A movie theater charges $9 for an adult's ticket and $5 for a child's ticket. On a recent night, the sale of child's tickets was two times the sale of adult's tickets. If the total amount collected for ticket sales was not more than $3,800, what is the greatest number of adults who could have purchased tickets? [Show or explain the procedure used to obtain your answer.] [10]

GRAPHING SYSTEMS OF INEQUALITIES

Example:

a. On the same set of coordinate axes, graph the following system of inequalities:

$y < -x + 8$ $\qquad$ $y \geq \frac{5}{3}x$ $\qquad$ [8]

b. Label the solution set S [1]

c. Write the coordinates of a point in the solution set of the graph drawn in answer to part a. [1]

Solution:

1) Rewrite the inequalities solving for y in terms of x, if necessary.
REMEMBER: Dividing by a negative or multiplying by a negative value changes the order of the inequality.

2) Select values for x and solve for y.

x	-x + 8	y
0	0 + 8	8
1	-1 + 8	7
2	-2 + 8	6
3	-3 + 8	5

x	$\frac{5}{3}x$	y
0	$\frac{5}{3}(0)$	0
3	$\frac{5}{3}(3)$	5
6	$\frac{5}{3}(6)$	10

3) Graph the two inequalities.
REMEMBER: use a solid line for $\geq$ or $\leq$ and use a dash line for $>$ or $<$.

4) Test for region of crosshatch:
Use (0,0) for $y < -x + 8$
$\qquad 0 < 0 + 8$
(0,0) in HALF-PLANE since $0 < 8$ true

Use (3,0) for $y \geq \frac{5}{3}x$
$\qquad 0 \geq \frac{5}{3}(3)$
$\qquad 0 \not\geq 5$

(3,0) not in HALF-PLANE since
$\qquad 0 \geq 5$ false

5) There are many points in the solution set. One acceptable answer is (1,4).

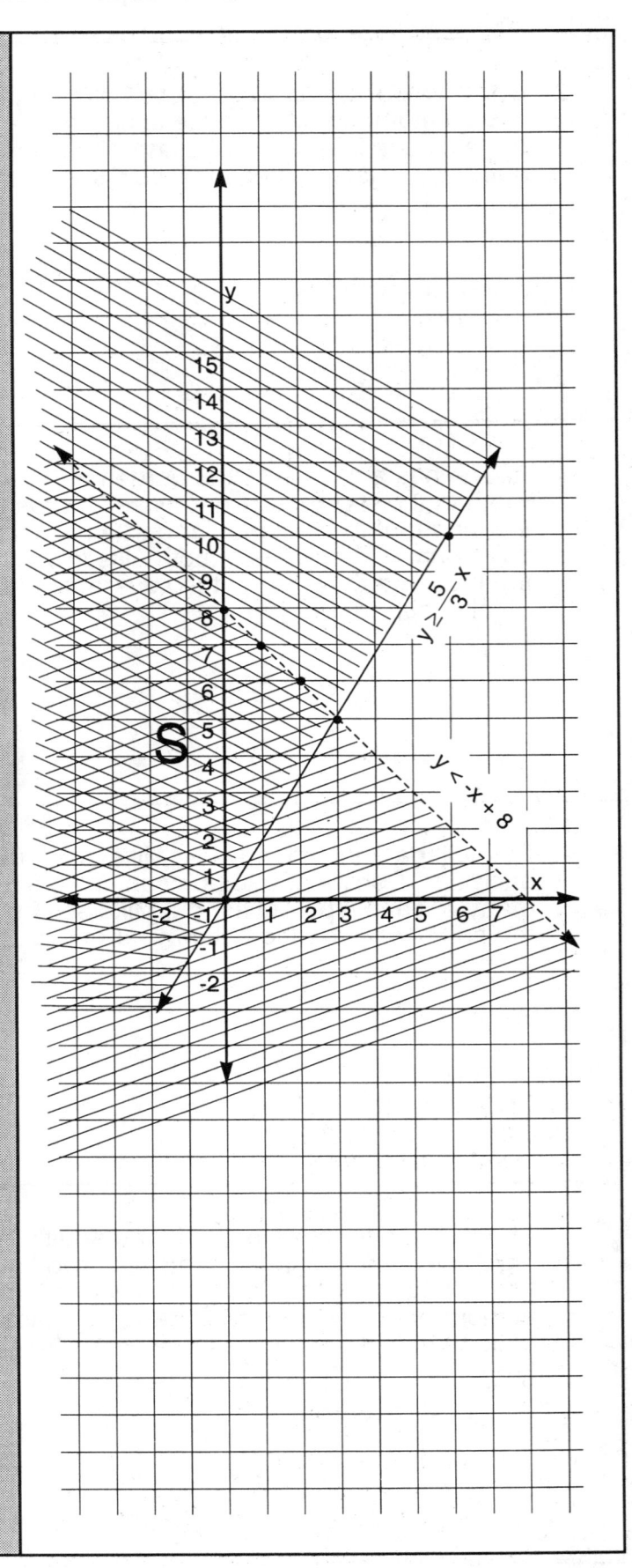

GRAPHING SYSTEMS OF INEQUALITIES

(Continued)

1a. On the same set of coordinate axes, graph the following system of inequalities:

$$y \geq 4x + 2$$
$$x + y > 6$$

[8]

b. Based on your answer to part a., write the coordinates of a point which is NOT in the solution set of the system of inequalities. [1]

c. Based on your answer to part a., write the coordinates of a point which IS in the solution set of the system of inequalities. [1]

2a. On the same set of coordinate axes, graph the following system of inequalities:

$$x - 4y < 8$$
$$y \leq 1 - x$$

[8]

b. Based on your answer to part a., write the coordinates of a point which is NOT in the solution set of the system of inequalities. [1]

c. Based on your answer to part a., write the coordinates of a point which IS in the solution set of the system of inequalities. [1]

3a. On the same set of coordinate axes, graph the following system of inequalities and label the solution set A:

$$y > -4 \quad \text{and} \quad y \geq 2x - 4$$

[8]

b. A point in the solution set is:
(1) (0,0)   (3) (0,-4)
(2) (4,0)   (4) (-4,-4)

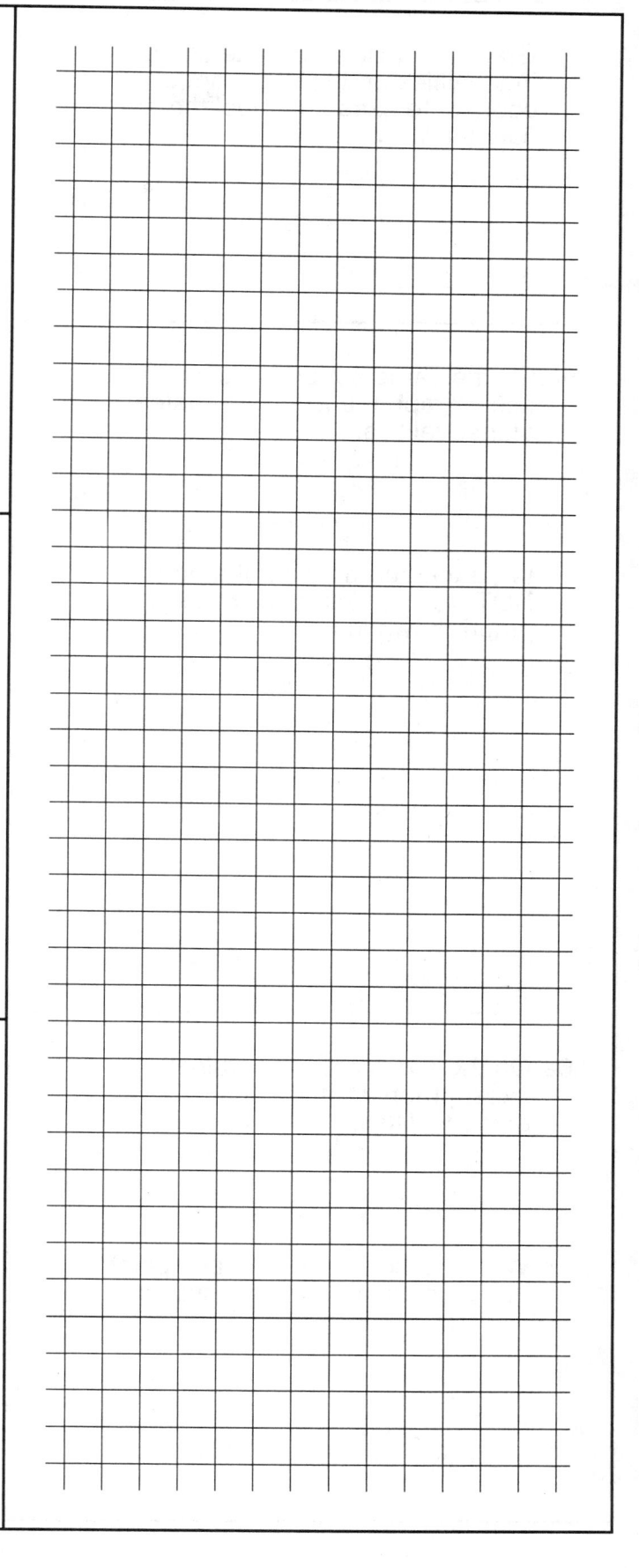

GRAPHING SYSTEMS OF INEQUALITIES

(Continued)

4. Graph the following systems of inequalities on the same set of coordinate axes and label the solution set A.

$$x + y < 4$$
$$y \leq 5x$$

[8,2]

5a. On the same set of coordinate axes, graph the following system of inequalities:

$$y \leq -3x + 5$$
$$x - y > 2$$

[8]

b. Write the coordinates of a point NOT in the solution set of the graph drawn in answer to part a.

[2]

6a. On the same set of coordinate axes, graph the following system of inequalities:

$$y > -2x + 6$$
$$y \geq 3x - 4$$

[8]

b. Write the coordinates of any point in the solution set of this system.

[2]

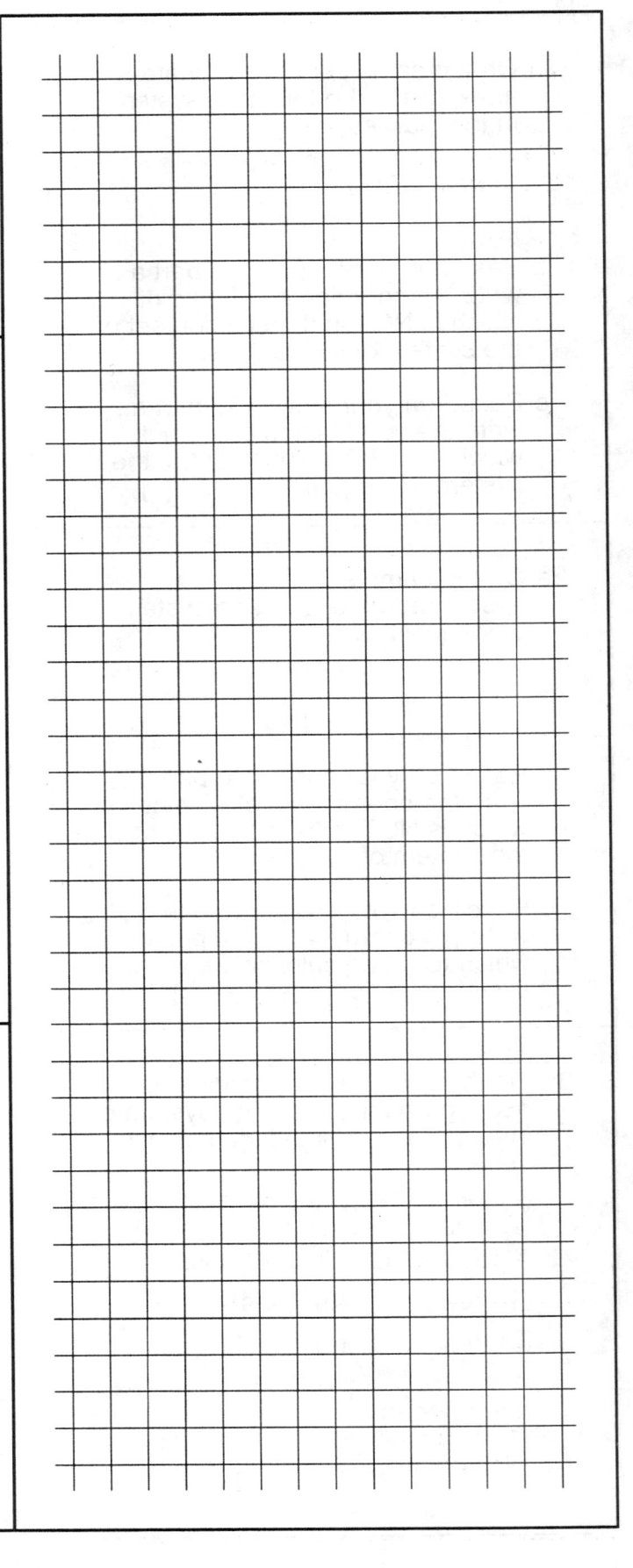

PERIMETERS OF POLYGONS

SAMPLE PROBLEM

The longer leg of a right triangle is 3 more than the shorter leg. The hypotenuse is 6 more than the shorter leg. If the perimeter of the triangle is 36, find the length of each side of the right triangle. [Only an algebraic solution will be accepted]   [5,5]

Solution:

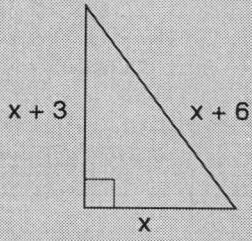

Legs labeled: $x+3$, $x+6$, and x (with right angle).

let shorter leg = x
and longer leg = x + 3
and hypotenuse = x + 6

The sum of the legs = perimeter

$$x + x + 3 + x + 6 = 36$$
$$3x + 9 = 36$$
$$3x = 36 - 9$$
$$\frac{3x}{3} = \frac{27}{3}$$
$$x = 9$$

x = 9 is shorter leg
x + 3 = 12 is longer leg
x + 6 = 15 is hypotenuse

CHECK:
sum of sides = perimeter
9 + 12 + 15 = 36
36 = 36

---

1. As shown in the accompanying figure, ABCD is a rectangle, E is a point on DC, AE = 26, DE = 10, AB = 35.
   a. Find side AD   [3]
   b. Find the value of segment EC   [1]
   c. Find the perimeter of triangle ADE   [2]
   d. Find the perimeter of trapezoid ABCE   [2]
   e. Find the perimeter of rectangle ABCD   [2]

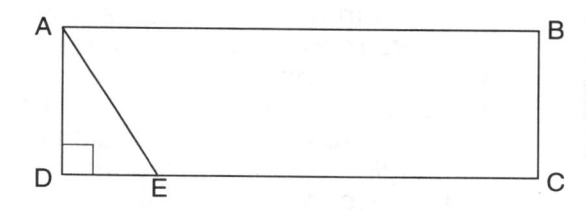

---

2. The length of a rectangle is ten more than five times the width. The perimeter of the rectangle is 152. Find the length and width of the rectangle. [Only an algebraic solution will be accepted]   [5,5]

---

3. The length of a rectangle is six more than one-half the width of the rectangle. If the perimeter of the rectangle is 72, find the length of a diagonal of the rectangle to the nearest tenth.   [5,5]

PERIMETERS OF POLYGONS

(Continued)

4. The length of a rectangle is three times the length of a side of a square and the width of the rectangle is two less than the side of the square. If the perimeter of the rectangle is twenty eight more than the perimeter of the square, find the length of a side of the square. [Only an algebraic solution will be accepted]   [5,5]

5. The length of a rectangle is five less than twice the width. If the perimeter of the rectangle is 80, find the numerical value of both the length and the width of the rectangle. [Only an algebraic solution will be accepted]   [5,5]

6. The length of a rectangle is two centimeters more than three times the width. If the perimeter of the rectangle is 76 centimeters, find the number of centimeters in each dimension of the rectangle. [Only an algebraic solution will be accepted]   [5,5]

7. The legs of a right triangle are represented by x and x + 7. The hypotenuse is 13.

   a. Find x [Only an algebraic solution will be accepted]   [8]

   b. Find the perimeter of the triangle.   [2]

PERIMETERS OF POLYGONS
(Continued)

8. The base of an isosceles triangle is four less than the sum of the lengths of the two legs. If the perimeter of the triangle is 44, find the length of the three sides of the triangle. [Only an algebraic solution will be accepted] [5,5]

9. In the accompanying diagram, ABDE is a rectangle, ABCE is a trapezoid, EC:DC = 3:1, EC = 24, BC = 17 and the perimeter of rectangle ABDE is 62. Find:
   a. DC   [4]
   b. ED   [1]
   c. AB   [1]
   d. BD   [2]
   e. perimeter of triangle BCD   [2]

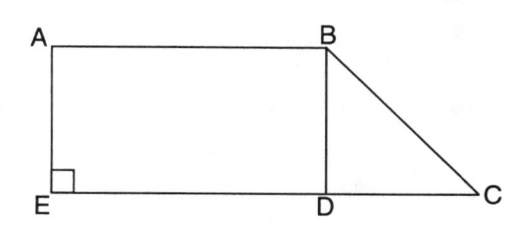

10. The length of a side of a square is fifteen less than four times the length of a side of a second square. The perimeter of the two squares differ by 24 inches. Find in inches, the length of a side of the smaller square. [Only an algebraic solution will be accepted] [6,4]

11. A storage shed is in the shape of a square. A builder increases the length of one side of the shed by three feet and decreases the length of an adjacent side by two feet. The shed is now a rectangle with a perimeter of 70 feet. What is the measure of a side of the original shed? [Only an algebraic solution will be accepted]   [5,5]

AREA OF POLYGONS

Important Area Formulas:

Square: $A = s^2$
Rectangle: $A = lw$ or $A = bh$
Triangle: $A = \frac{1}{2}bh$

Parallelogram: $A = bh$
Trapezoid: $A = \frac{1}{2}h(b_1 + b_2)$

Example: The length of a rectangle is 9 more than the side of a square. The width of the rectangle is equal to the side of the square. The area of the square is 63 less than the area of the rectangle. Find the side of the square. [Only an algebraic solution will be accepted.]

Solution: Let x = side of the square
Let x + 9 = length of the rectangle

Area of Square = s^2
Area of Rectangle = lw

[Rectangle with width x and length x+9; Square with side x]

$x^2 = x(x+9) - 63$
$x^2 = x^2 + 9x - 63$
$63 = 9x$
$x = 7$ side of the square **Ans.**

1. A garden is in the shape of a square. The length of one side of the garden is increased by one foot and the length of an adjacent side is decreased by 4 feet. The garden now has an area of 50 square feet. What is the measure of a side of the original garden? [Only an algebraic solution will be accepted] [5,5]

2. The measure of the base of a parallelogram is 3 meters more than the measure of the altitude to that base. If the area of the parallelogram is 40 square meters, find the number of meters in the measures of the base and altitude. [Only an algebraic solution will be accepted]   [5,5]

3. In a trapezoid, the smaller base is 6 more than the height, the larger base is 2 less than 5 times the height, and the area of the trapezoid is 85 square centimeters. Find in centimeters, the height of the trapezoid. [Only an algebraic solution will be accepted] [5,5]

AREA OF POLYGONS
(Continued)

4. In the accompanying figure, quadrilateral ABCD is a trapezoid with AB ∥ DC, AD⊥AB, AB = AD = 6, DB⊥BC, and DC = 10.
   a. Find DB in radical form   [3]
   b. Find the area of triangle ABD   [2]
   c. Find the area of trapezoid ABCD   [3]
   d. Find the area of triangle DBC   [2]

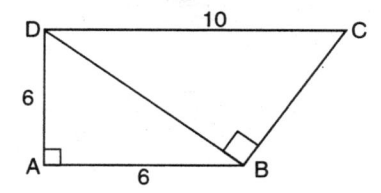

5. In the accompanying diagram, ABCD is a rectangle and DEFG is a square. The area of ABCD is 63, CG = 4, and AE = 6. Find the length of the side of square DEFG. [Only an algebraic solution will be accepted.]   [5,5]

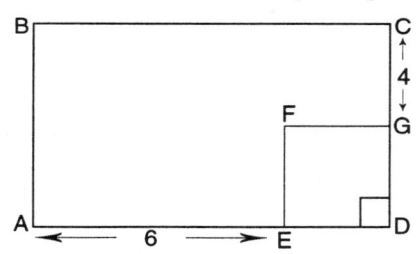

6. As shown in the accompanying diagram, ABCD is a rectangle and a line segment drawn from B intersects $\overline{CD}$ at E.
   a. If the measure of $\overline{AB}$ is 12 and the area of the rectangle is 60, find AD. [2]
   b. The point E separates $\overline{DC}$ into two segments each such that DE:EC = 2:1. Find DE and EC.   [2]
   c. Find BE in radical form.   [3]
   d. Find the area of trapezoid ABED.   [3]

AREA AND CIRCUMFERENCE OF THE CIRCLE

In the accompanying diagram, AD is the diameter pf circle O, BC is a diameter of circle Q, ABCD is a square and side AB = 20. [Answers may be left in terms of π.]

Find:
a. the circumference of circle O. [2]
b. the area of circle O. [2]
c. the area of semicircle Q. [2]
d. the area of square ABCD. [2]
e. the area of the shaded portion. [2]

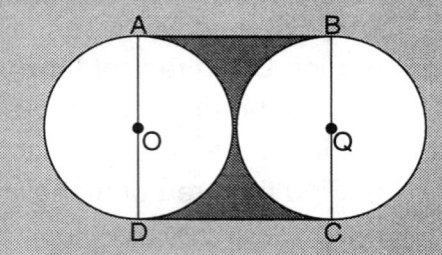

Solution:

a. $C = \pi d$. Since ABCD is a square, AB = AD = 20
   $C = 20\pi$. Answer

b. $A = \pi r^2$. Since the radius = $\frac{1}{2}$ the diameter, $r = \frac{1}{2}(20) = 10$
   $A = \pi 10^2 = 100\pi$ Answer

c. Since the circles O and Q have equal diameters, the area of the semicircle is $\frac{1}{2}(100\pi) = 50\pi$ Answer

d. The area of a square = $S^2 = (20)(20) = 400$ Answer

e. The area of the shaded portion is found by subtracting the area of a circle from the area of the square.
   Area of the shaded portion = $400 - 100\pi$ Answer

---

1. In the accompanying diagram, $\triangle$ ABC is inscribed in circle O with diameter $\overline{AC}$. Radius $\overline{OB}$ is an altitude of $\triangle$ ABC and OB = 8.
   a. Find AC. [2]
   b. Express the area of circle O in terms of π. [2]
   c. Find the area of $\triangle$ ABC. [2]
   d. Express in terms of π, the area of the shaded region. [2]
   e. Find BC. [Answer may be left in radical form. [2]

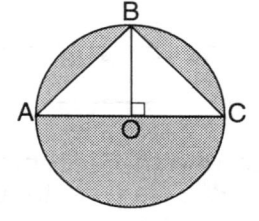

2. In the accompanying figure, rectangle ABCD is inscribed in circle O and $\overline{DB}$ is a diameter. The radius of the circle is 13. [Answers may be left in terms of π.]
   a. Find the area of the circle. [2]
   b. If CD = 24, find BC. [3]
   c. Find the area of $\triangle$ BCD. [2]
   d. Find the area of rectangle ABCD. [1]
   e. Find the area of the shaded portion of the figure. [2]

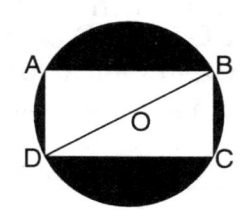

AREA AND CIRCUMFERENCE OF THE CIRCLE
(Continued)

3. Given: Rectangle ABCD with two circles removed from the rectangle. The length of the rectangle is 50 and its width is 20. The diameter of each circle is 10. [Answers may be left in terms of π.]
   a. What is the perimeter of the rectangle? [2]
   b. What is the circumference of either circle? [2]
   c. What is the area of the rectangle? [2]
   d. What is the area of either circle? [2]
   e. What is the area of the shaded portion of the diagram? [2]

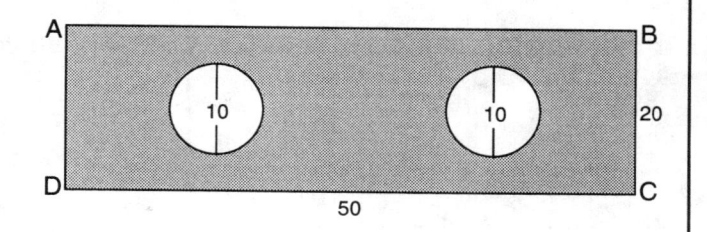

4. In the accompanying figure, square ABCD is circumscribed about circle O. The length of a side of the square and the diameter of the circle are both 12. [Answers may be left in terms of π.]
   a. What is the circumference of the circle? [2]
   b. What is the perimeter of the square? [2]
   c. What is the area of the square? [2]
   d. What is the area of the circle? [2]
   e. What is the area of the shaded portion of the diagram? [2]

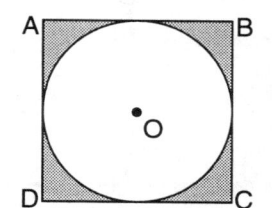

5. In the accompanying diagram, ABCD is a rectangle. Diameter $\overline{XY}$ of circle O is perpendicular to $\overline{BC}$ at X and to $\overline{AD}$ at Y. AD = 12 and CD = 9. [Answers may be left in terms of π.]
   a. What is the perimeter of rectangle ABCD? [2]
   b. What is the circumference of circle O? [2]
   c. What is the area of rectangle ABCD? [2]
   d. What is the area of circle O? [2]
   e. What is the area of the shaded region of the diagram? [2]

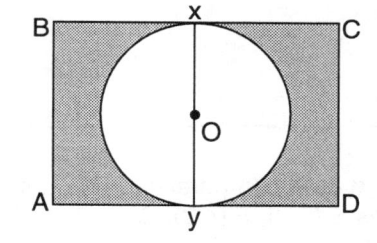

6. The accompanying figure shows two circles with the same center. The radii of the circles are 5 and 8, respectively. [Answers may be left in terms of π.]
   a. Find the area of the larger circle. [2]
   b. Find the area of the smaller circle. [2]
   c. Find the area of the shaded portion. [2]
   d. What fraction of the diagram is unshaded? [2]
   e. If the radius of a circle is doubled, the area of the circle is:
      (1) squared   (3) multiplied by 8
      (2) doubled   (4) multiplied by 4   [2]

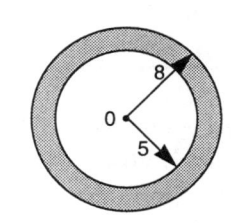

AREA OF POLYGONS

Find the area of the six sided polygon whose vertices are Q(2,6), R(6,6), S(8,0), T(6,-6), U(2,-6), V(0,0).   [10]

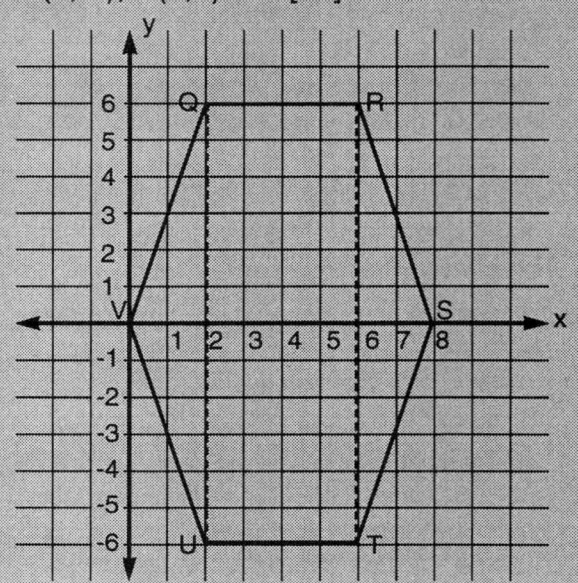

Solution:
To find the area, divide the polygon up into a rectangle and two triangles. Draw segments QU and RT to form rectangle QRTU and triangles QVU and RST.

Rectangle QRTU has a length RT = 12 and width QR = 4. Area = l x w = 12 x 4 = 48. Triangle QVU has a base QU = 12 and height = 2.
Area = $\frac{1}{2}$ base x height. Area = $\frac{1}{2}$ x 12 x 2 = 12.
Triangle RST has a base RT = 12 and height = 2.
Area = $\frac{1}{2}$ x 12 x 2 = 12.

Adding all the areas 48 + 12 + 12 = 72. Ans.

1. Find the area of a rectangle with vertices A (-2,2), B (3,2), C (3, -3) and D (-2,-3).   [10]

2. Find the area of a parallelogram EFGH with vertices E (0,2), F (4,2), G (2,-2) and H (-2,-2).   [10]

3. Find the area of triangle IJK whose vertices are I (0,0), J (0,4) and K (6,0).   [10]

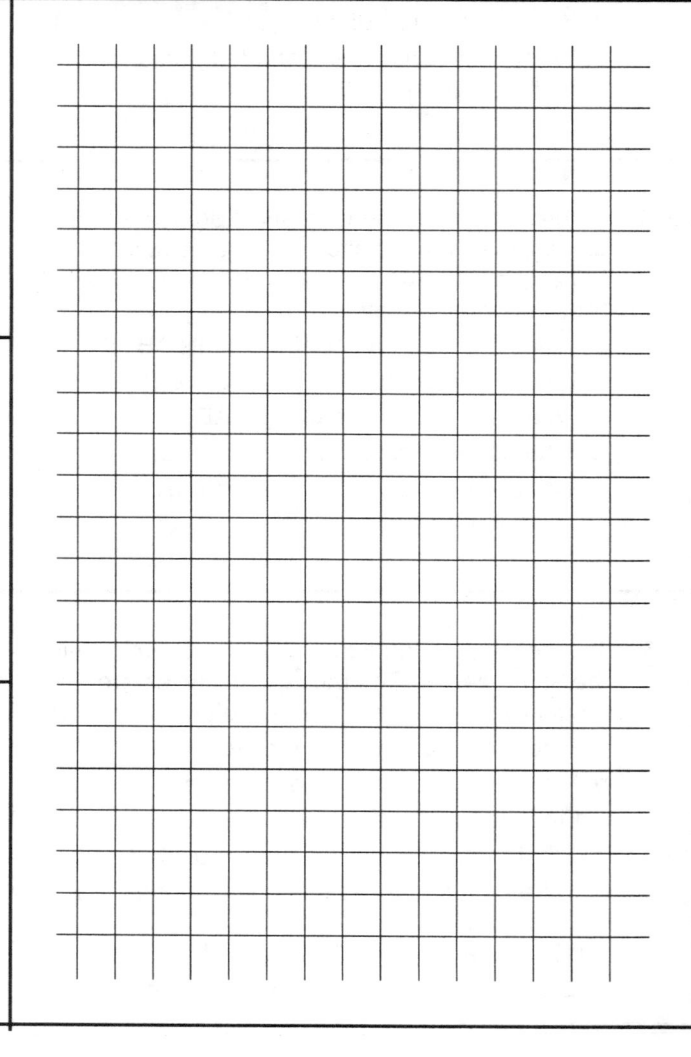

AREA OF POLYGONS

(Continued)

4. Find the area of trapezoid LMPN with vertices L (0,0), M (2,4), N (6,0) and P (4,4). [10]

5. a. On the same set of coordinate axes, graph the following equations:
   $$x = 2$$
   $$y = x + 3$$
   $$x + y = 1$$ [7]

   b. Find the area of the triangle formed by lines graphed in part a. [3]

6. Find the area of quadrilateral ABCD whose vertices are A (1,3), B (5,3), C (5,-2) and D (-2,0). [10]

7. Find the area of the eight sided polygon EFGHIJKL whose vertices are E (2,5), F (6,5), G (8,3), H (8,1), I (6,-2), J (2,-2), K (1,1) and L (1,3). [10]

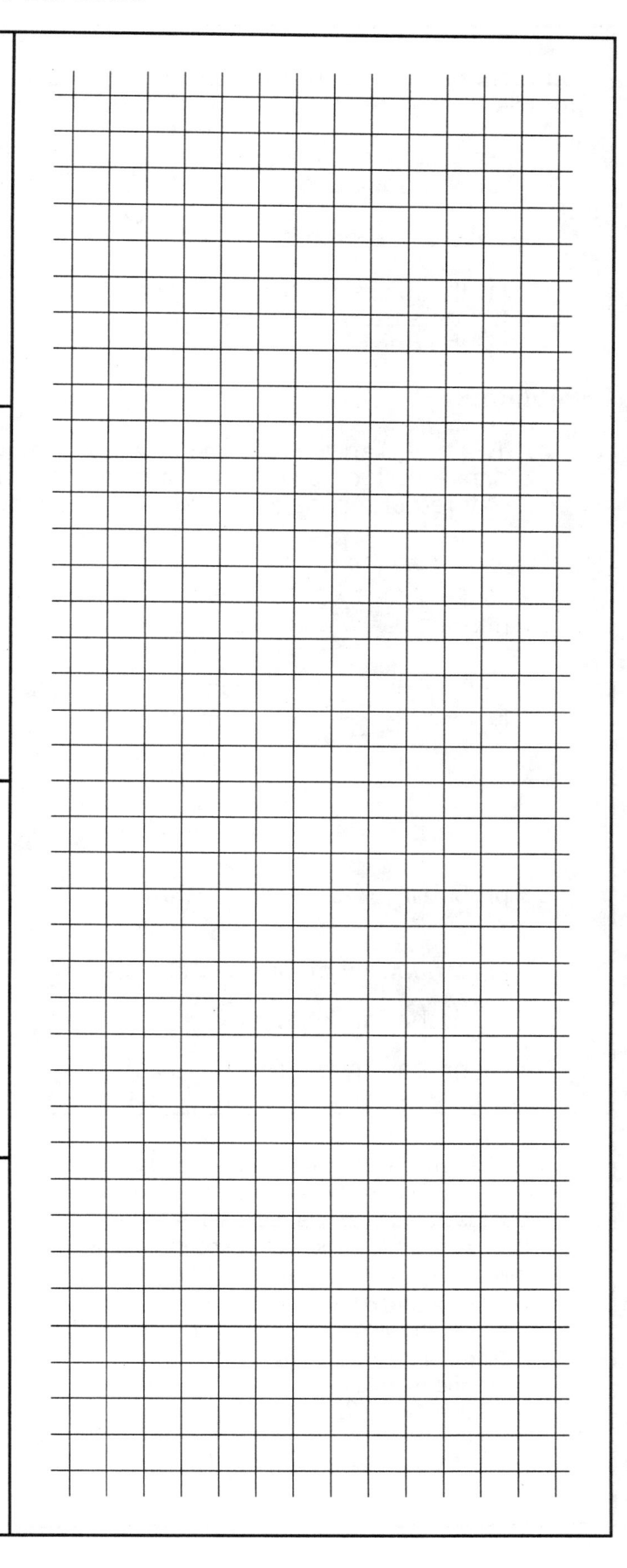

PROBABILITY

A student purchases lunch that consists of one drink and one sandwich. The drinks available are milk and juice. The sandwiches available are meat, cheese and jelly.

a. Make a tree diagram or list the sample space showing all possible lunch combinations for one drink and one sandwich. [4]

b. What is the probability that:

(1) the lunch consists of milk and a cheese sandwich? [2]
(2) the sandwich is meat? [2]
(3) the drink is juice? [2]

Solution:

a. The tree diagram will have branching in two directions to indicate the two choices of drinks: milk or juice. Each of these two initial branches then divides into a second set of three branches to indicate the three choices of sandwiches: meat, cheese or jelly.

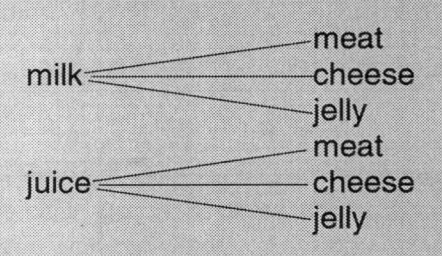

The sample space requires two columns to list the types of items.

milk — meat, cheese, jelly
juice — meat, cheese, jelly

DRINK CHOICE	SANDWICH CHOICE
milk	meat
milk	cheese
milk	jelly
juice	meat
juice	cheese
juice	jelly

b. probability of an event occurring = $\dfrac{\text{number of favorable outcomes}}{\text{total outcomes}}$

(1) probability of milk and cheese = $\dfrac{1}{6}$

(2) probability of meat = $\dfrac{2}{6} = \dfrac{1}{3}$

(3) probability of juice = $\dfrac{3}{6} = \dfrac{1}{2}$

---

1. A bag contains 3 green marbles, and 2 white marbles. One marble is randomly selected, its color is noted, and it is replaced. A second marble is randomly selected and its color is noted.

   a. Make a tree diagram or list the sample space showing all possible outcomes. [4]
   b. Find the probability that:
   (1) one marble is white and the other is green. [2]
   (2) neither marble is white. [2]
   (3) at least one marble is white. [2]

PROBABILITY

(Continued)

2. If it does not rain on Saturday nor on Sunday, Dianne and Maureen will go jogging. The probability of raining on Saturday is $\frac{2}{9}$ and the probability of raining on Sunday is $\frac{3}{7}$. What is the probability of:

   a. not raining on Saturday? [2]

   b. not raining on Saturday and raining on Sunday? [2]

   c. jogging on Sunday after already jogging on Saturday? [2]

   d. raining on both days? [2]

   e. not raining on either day? [2]

3. The Computer Club wants to elect a chairperson and a treasurer. Alice, Bob and Clare are candidates for chairperson. Donna, Ed and Frank are candidates for treasurer.

   a. Make a tree diagram or write a sample space of all possible pairs of candidates, consisting of a chairperson and a treasurer that could be elected. [2]

   b. If each person is equally likely to be elected, find the probability that:
      (1) a boy and a girl are elected. [2]
      (2) two boys are elected. [2]
      (3) Bob is elected chairperson. [2]
      (4) Ed is elected treasurer. [2]

4. A fair die and a fair coin are tossed.

   a. Draw a tree diagram or list the sample space of all possible pairs of outcomes. [4]

   b. What is the probability of obtaining a 4 on the die and a head on the coin? [2]

   c. What is the probability of obtaining an odd number on the die and a tail on the coin? [2]

   d. What is the probability of obtaining a 2 on the die or a head on the coin? [2]

PROBABILITY
(Continued)

5. The letters B, I, R, D are written on four individual cards and placed in a container. Each has an equal likelihood of being drawn. One card is drawn from the container, the letter noted, and then the card is returned to the container. A second card is drawn and the letter noted.

   a. Make a tree diagram or list the sample space showing all possible outcomes after both drawings.   [4]
   b. Find the probability that:
      (1) the first letter drawn is I and the second letter is B   [2]
      (2) for both drawings the letter R does not appear   [2]
      (3) both letters drawn are D   [2]

6. A nickel, a dime and a quarter are in a box. Mike randomly selects a coin, notes its value and returns it to the box. He randomly selects another coin from the box.

   a. Draw a tree diagram or list the sample space showing all possible outcomes.   [4]
   b. What is the probability that a dime will be drawn more than once?   [2]
   c. What is the probability that the total value of both coins which were selected will be less than 15¢?   [2]
   d. What is the probability that a quarter will be drawn at least once?   [2]

7. The diagram represents an arrow attached to a cardboard disc. The arrow is free to spin, but can not land on a line. The disc is divided into six regions of equal area, one of which is black, two red, and three white.

   a. For any one spin, what is the probability of the arrow:
      (1) landing on white?   [1]
      (2) landing on black?   [1]

   b. The arrow is spun twice and each outcome is recorded. What is the probability of the arrow:
      (1) landing in red on the first spin and white on the second spin?   [2]
      (2) landing on black on both spins?   [2]
      (3) not landing on black on either spin?   [2]
      (4) landing on the same color on both spins?   [2]

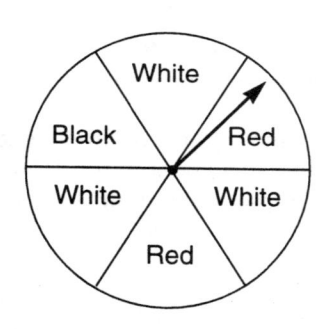

132

PROBABILITY
(Continued)

8. Each card below is printed with either a vowel (A, E, I, O, or U) or a consonant (a letter other than a vowel). The cards are either plain or striped.

   [Cards: C (striped), O (plain), M (striped), P (striped), U (plain), T (striped), E (striped), R (striped)]

   a. The cards are shuffled and a card is drawn at random. Find the probability that the card will be:
      (1) a vowel [1]   (2) striped and a vowel [2]   (3) striped or a vowel [2]

   b. One card is drawn and the letter is noted. The card is not replaced and a second card is drawn. Find the probability that both cards drawn will be vowels. [2]

   c. Two cards are drawn with replacement. What is the probability that the two cards drawn will both be vowels? [3]

9. Without looking, Allison chooses one block from a box containing four blocks numbered 1 through 4. Next she chooses one block from a second box containing four blocks lettered A, B, C, and D.

   a. Draw a tree diagram or list the sample space of all possible outcomes. [3]

   b. Find the probability that Allison chose:
      (1) an even number   [1]
      (2) an odd number and the letter A   [2]
      (3) a number greater than 3 or the letter B   [2]
      (4) a number less than 3 and a letter from the word "BADGE"   [2]

10. A can contains a total of 28 marbles that are red, white, or blue. The number of white marbles is five more than the number of red marbles, and the number of blue marbles is one less than twice the number of red marbles.

    a. How many marbles of each color are in the jar?   [5]

    b. One marble is randomly selected, its color is noted, and it is returned to the jar. A second marble is randomly selected and its color is noted. Find the probability that:

       (1) both marbles selected are red   [2]
       (2) the first marble selected is blue and the second marble selected is white   [2]
       (3) one of the marbles selected is white   [1]

TRANSFORMATIONS

1. For each example in the left column, choose the expression from the right column that best describes the example. Then write the **numeral** of the expression next to the letter.   [10]

   a. An isosceles trapezoid

   b. Z

   c. 5 by 7 photograph → 10 by 14 enlargement

   d. (triangle → translated triangle)

   e. (house reflected across line ℓ)

   (1) Has exactly one line of symmetry

   (2) Illustrates a dilation

   (3) Illustrates a translation

   (4) Has point symmetry

   (5) Has two lines of symmetry

   (6) Illustrates a rotation

   (7) Illustrates a line reflection

   a_____   b_____   c_____   d_____   e_____

2. For each example in the left column, choose the expression from the right column that best describes the example. Then write the **numeral** of the expression next to the letter.   [10]

   a. A rhombus

   b. E

   c. (triangle → smaller triangle)

   d. P → ꟼ

   e. (4,8) •
      • (8,4)
      (line m)

   (1) Has exactly one line of symmetry

   (2) Illustrates a dilation

   (3) Illustrates a translation

   (4) Has point symmetry

   (5) Has two lines of symmetry

   (6) Illustrates a rotation

   (7) Illustrates a line reflection

   a_____   b_____   c_____   d_____   e_____

TRANSFORMATIONS
(Continued)

3. On your answer sheet write the letters **a, b, c, d** and **e**. Then next to each letter write the numeral that best describes the answer to the problem.

    a. If a rectangle is **not** square, what is the greatest number of lines of symmetry that can be drawn? [2]
       (1) 1   (2) 2   (3) 3   (4) 4

    b. Which letter has vertical but **not** horizontal symmetry? [2]
       (1) B   (2) M   (3) S   (4) X

    c. Under which transformation can the image be a different size than the original figure? [2]
       (1) reflection   (2) dilation   (3) translation   (4) rotation

    d. Which figures have both point symmetry and line symmetry? [2]

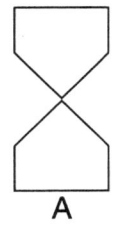

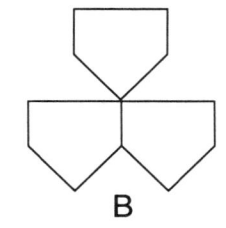

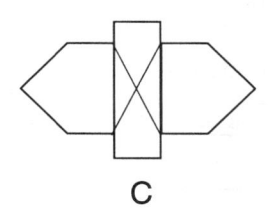

       (1) A, B, and C
       (2) A and C, only
       (3) A and B, only
       (4) B and C, only

    e. In the accompanying diagram, △A'B'C' is the image of △ABC. Which type of transformation is represented by △A'B'C'? [2]

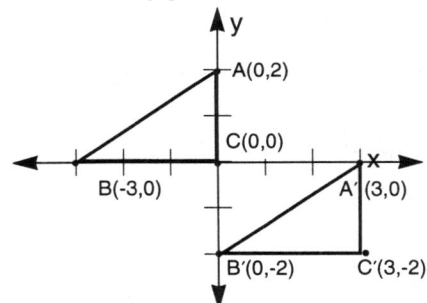

       (1) reflection
       (2) dilation
       (3) translation
       (4) rotation

       a) _____
       b) _____
       c) _____
       d) _____
       e) _____

135

QUARTILES AND PERCENTILES

The 50th percentile is the median. Half the data is larger and half the data is smaller.

The 75th percentile is the upper quartile. This data is the top 25% of the values.

The 25th percentile is the lower quartile. This data is the bottom 25% of the values.

The total frequency is found by adding the frequency column.

1. The following data represent the heights of 20 students in a certain class: 58, 60, 65, 59, 61, 64, 62, 63, 63, 64, 68, 66, 59, 64, 61, 65, 63, 60, 66, 64.

   a. On your answer paper, copy and complete the table. [2]
   b. Find the mean. (to the nearest 10th) [4]
   c. Find the median. [2]
   d. Find the mode. [2]

Height	Number (frequency)
58	
59	
60	
61	
62	
63	
64	
65	
66	
67	
68	

2. The HI-TECH COMPANY, maker of electronic games, listed the following salaries in its annual report:

Employee	Position	Salary
Al Able	Manager	$70,000
Bob Baker	Accountant	90,000
Carol Collins	Foreman	47,000
Dave Daniels	Technician	32,000
Ellen Evans	Wire Person	26,000
Frank Fink	Electrician	47,000
George Gross	Solderer	17,000
Harry Holt	Secretary	22,000
Inez Izzo	Custodian	20,000

   a. Using all nine salaries,
      (1) find the mean to the nearest thousand dollars [3]
      (2) find the median [3]
      (3) find the mode [1]

   b. How much more than the mean in part a is the manager's salary? [1]

   c. If an employee is selected at random, what is the probability that this person's salary is greater than the mean? [2]

QUARTILES AND PERCENTILES
(Continued)

3. The data at the right represent the distribution of test grades of students on a math test.

   a. Find the total frequency. [2]

   b. Find the mode. [2]

   c. Find the median. [2]

   d. Find the mean. (to the nearest 10th) [4]

Grade	Number (frequency)
60	2
65	1
70	0
75	3
80	4
85	2
90	2
95	0
100	1

4. On a quiz, 15 students received the following grades: 23, 20, 22, 24, 23, 25, 21, 21, 22, 19, 23, 18, 24, 22, 23.

   a. On your answer paper, copy and complete the tables below. [3]

Grades	Frequency
18 - 19	
20 - 21	
22 - 23	
24 - 25	

Grades	Cumulative Frequency
18 - 19	
18 - 21	
18 - 23	
18 - 25	

   b. Find the median. [2]
   c. Find the mode. [2]
   d. Find the 75th percentile. [3]

5. The diagram below is a cumulative frequency histogram of raw scores on a mathematics examination.

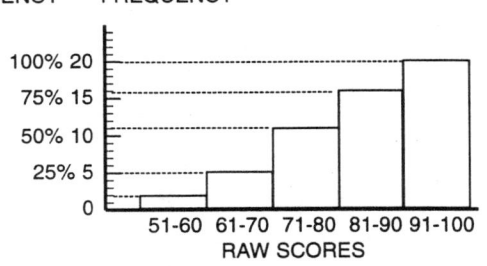

   a. How many students took the examination? [2]
   b. How many students had a score less than or equal to 90? [2]
   c. What percent of the students had a score less than or equal to 90? [2]
   d. Which interval contains the median? [2]
   e. Which interval contains the lower quartile? [2]

137

FREQUENCY HISTOGRAMS

The following table represents the age in years of used automobiles advertised in a local daily newspaper.

Using the data in the Frequency column of the table, draw a histogram. [10]

Age Interval	Frequency
1 or less	6
2 - 6	20
7 - 11	14
12 - 16	8
17 or more	2

SOLUTION:

Step 1. Draw and label a vertical axis to show NUMBER OF AUTOMOBILES. The scale starts at 0 and increases by 2 to include the largest value (frequency in any one interval).

Step 2. Draw and label a horizontal axis to show AGE IN YEARS intervals.

Step 3. Draw vertical bars for each interval. Note that there are no spaces between bars and the first bar is not touching the vertical axis. Each bar stops at its Frequency value.

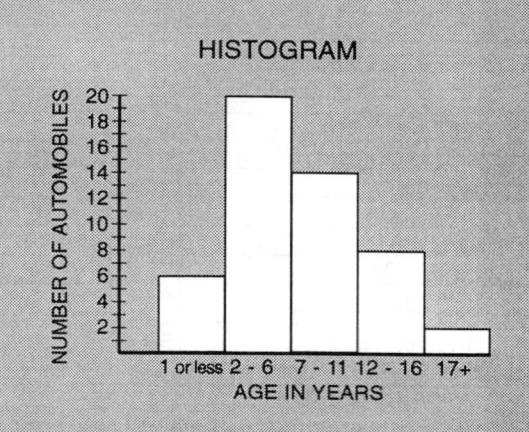

1. The following data represents the heights of 15 students in a certain class: 63, 59, 71, 63, 59, 68, 61, 60, 69, 55, 64, 70, 64, 68, 72.

    a. On your answer paper, copy and complete the table. [2]

Interval	Number (frequency)
55-57	
58-60	
61-63	
64-66	
67-69	
70-72	

    b. On graph paper, construct a frequency histogram based on the data. [6]

    c. The median is contained in which interval? [2]

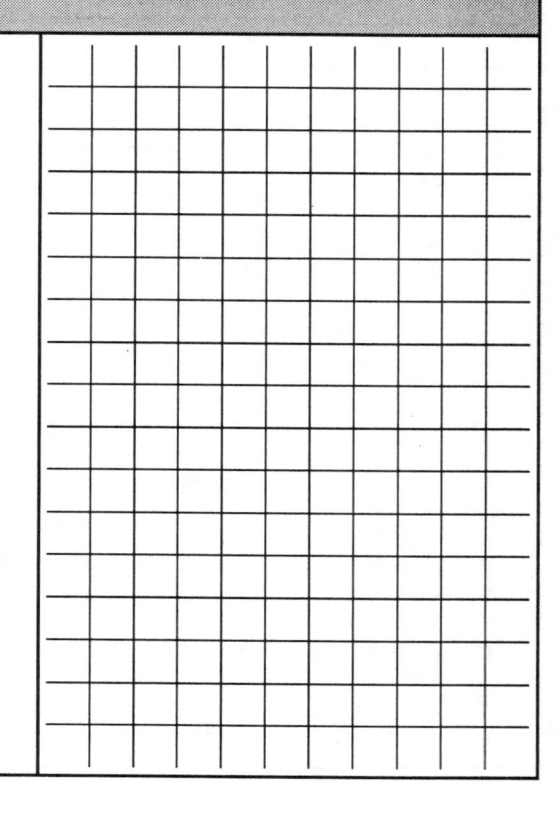

138

FREQUENCY HISTOGRAMS
(Continued)

2. The following data are test scores for a class of 20 students: 83, 91, 77, 88, 80, 62, 55, 92, 58, 96, 88, 60, 89, 100, 87, 64, 98, 88, 86, 70.

   a. On your answer paper copy and complete the following table. [2]

Interval	Number (frequency)
91-100	
81-90	
71-80	
61-70	
51-60	

   b. On graph paper, construct a frequency histogram based on the data. [4]

   c. Which interval contains the median? [2]

   d. Which interval contains the lower quartile? [1]

   e. What percent of the students scored less than 71? [1]

3. A class record showed the following number of grammatical errors in each of 20 term papers.

Errors	Frequency (Number of term papers)
0	0
1	1
2	2
3	3
4	4
5	4
6	6

   a. On graph paper, construct a frequency histogram based on the data. [3]

   b. Find the mean number of errors. (to the nearest 10th) [3]

   c. Find the median number of errors. [2]

   d. Find the mode number of errors. [2]

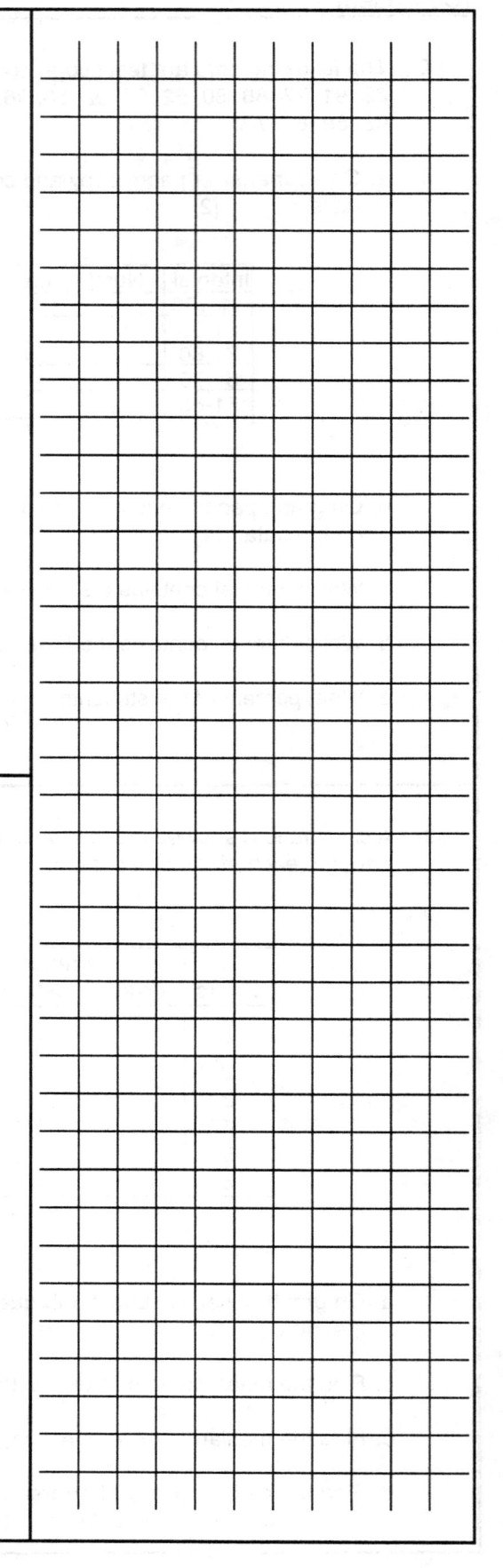

FREQUENCY HISTOGRAMS
(Continued)

4. The following data represent the examination marks of 14 students in a certain class: 87, 69, 90, 71, 80, 84, 83, 81, 86, 90, 99, 89, 78, 69.

   a. On your answer paper, copy and complete the table.   [2]

Interval	Number (frequency)
65-73	
74-82	
83-91	
92-100	

   b. On graph paper, construct a frequency histogram based on the data.   [6]

   c. The median is contained in which interval?   [1]

   d. What percent of the students earned marks greater than 83?   [1]

5. The table below gives the distribution of test scores for a class of 20 students.

Test Score Interval	Number of Students (frequency)
91-100	1
81-90	2
71-80	8
61-70	5
51-60	4

   a. Draw a frequency histogram for the given data.   [4]

   b. Which interval contains the median?   [2]

   c. Which interval contains the lower quartile?   [2]

   d. What is the probability that a student selected at random scored above 90?   [2]

140

CUMULATIVE FREQUENCY HISTOGRAMS

The following table represents the age in years of used automobiles advertised in a local daily newspaper:

Age Interval	Frequency
0 - 1	6
2 - 6	20
7 - 11	14
12 - 16	8
17 - 21	2

Age Interval	Cumulative Frequency
0 - 1	6
0 - 6	
0 - 11	
0 - 16	
0 - 21	

a. Complete the Cumulative Frequency column.
b. Using the data in the Cumulative Frequency column of the table, draw a cumulative frequency histogram.
c. On the same set of axis as part b. above, draw a cumulative frequency polygon.
d. Use your results from part b. to answer the following questions:
   (1) In which interval does the median lie?
   (2) In which interval does the upper quartile lie?
   (3) Which interval contains the lower quartile?

Solution:

a.

Age Interval	Frequency
0 - 1	6
2 - 6	20
7 - 11	14
12 - 16	8
17 - 21	2

Age Interval	Cumulative Frequency
0 - 1	6
0 - 6	26
0 - 11	40
0 - 16	48
0 - 21	50

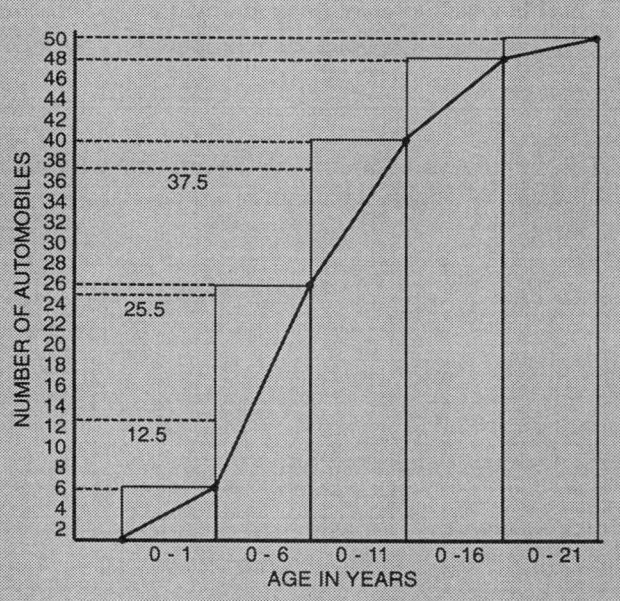

b. CUMULATIVE FREQUENCY HISTOGRAM (bars)

c. CUMULATIVE FREQUENCY POLYGON (line)

d. 1. The median (50th percentile) is the measure where 1/2 of the automobiles are older and 1/2 are newer. Since there are 50 automobiles, the median is between 25 and 26. Looking at the cumulative frequency histogram in part b., a value between 25 and 26 fails in the interval 0 - 6, the second bar. Therefore the answer is 0 - 6 age interval.

2. The upper quartile (75th percentile) is the top 25%. Since there are 50 automobiles, 25% would be 12.5. If we subtract 50 - 12.5, the result of 37.5 can be seen in the interval 0-11, the thrid bar. Therefore the answer is 0-11 age interval.

3. The lower quartile (25th percentile), 12.5 can be seen in the interval 0-6, the second bar. Therefore the answer is 0-6 age interval.

CUMULATIVE FREQUENCY HISTOGRAMS
(Continued)

1. The table below shows the distribution of bowling scores.

Interval	Frequency
91 - 110	4
111 - 130	10
131 - 150	15
151 - 170	6
171 - 190	1
191 - 210	3
211 - 230	1

Interval	Cumulative Frequency
91 - 110	4
91 - 130	
91 - 150	
91 - 170	
91 - 190	
91 - 210	
91 - 230	

a. Complete the Cumulative Frequency column above. [2]

b. Using the data in the Cumulative Frequency column of the table, draw a cumulative frequency histogram. [4]

c. Use your results from part b. to answer the following questions.

(1) In which interval does the median lie? [2]
(2) In which interval does the upper quartile lie? [2]

2. The cumulative frequency histogram below shows the number of weeks of annual vacation for workers at a company.

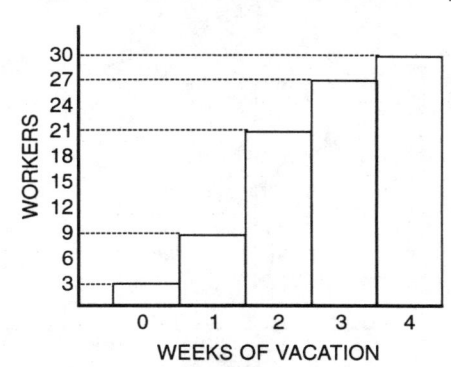

a. How many workers are employed by the company? [2]

b. How many workers receive more than 2 weeks vacation? [2]

c. Find the median number of weeks of vacation. [2]

d. Using the data from parts a, b, and c, draw a frequency histogram on your paper. [4]

142

CUMULATIVE FREQUENCY HISTOGRAMS

(Continued)

3. The frequency histogram below shows the distribution of scores on a science examination.

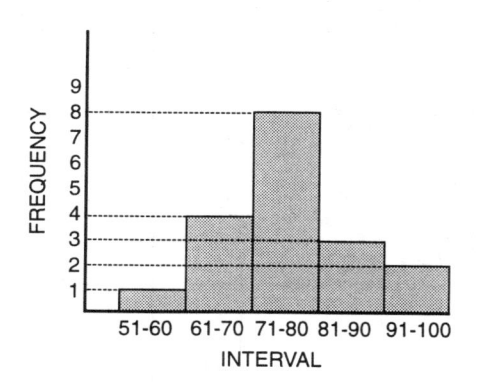

Scores	Frequency
51 - 60	
61 - 70	
71 - 80	
81 - 90	
91 - 100	

Scores	Cumulative Frequency
51 - 60	
51 - 70	
51 - 80	
51 - 90	
51 - 100	

a. On your answer paper, copy and complete the tables. [2]

b. How many students took the math test? [2]

c. How many students scored above 90? [2]

d. Using the table completed in part a, draw a cumulative frequency histogram. [4]

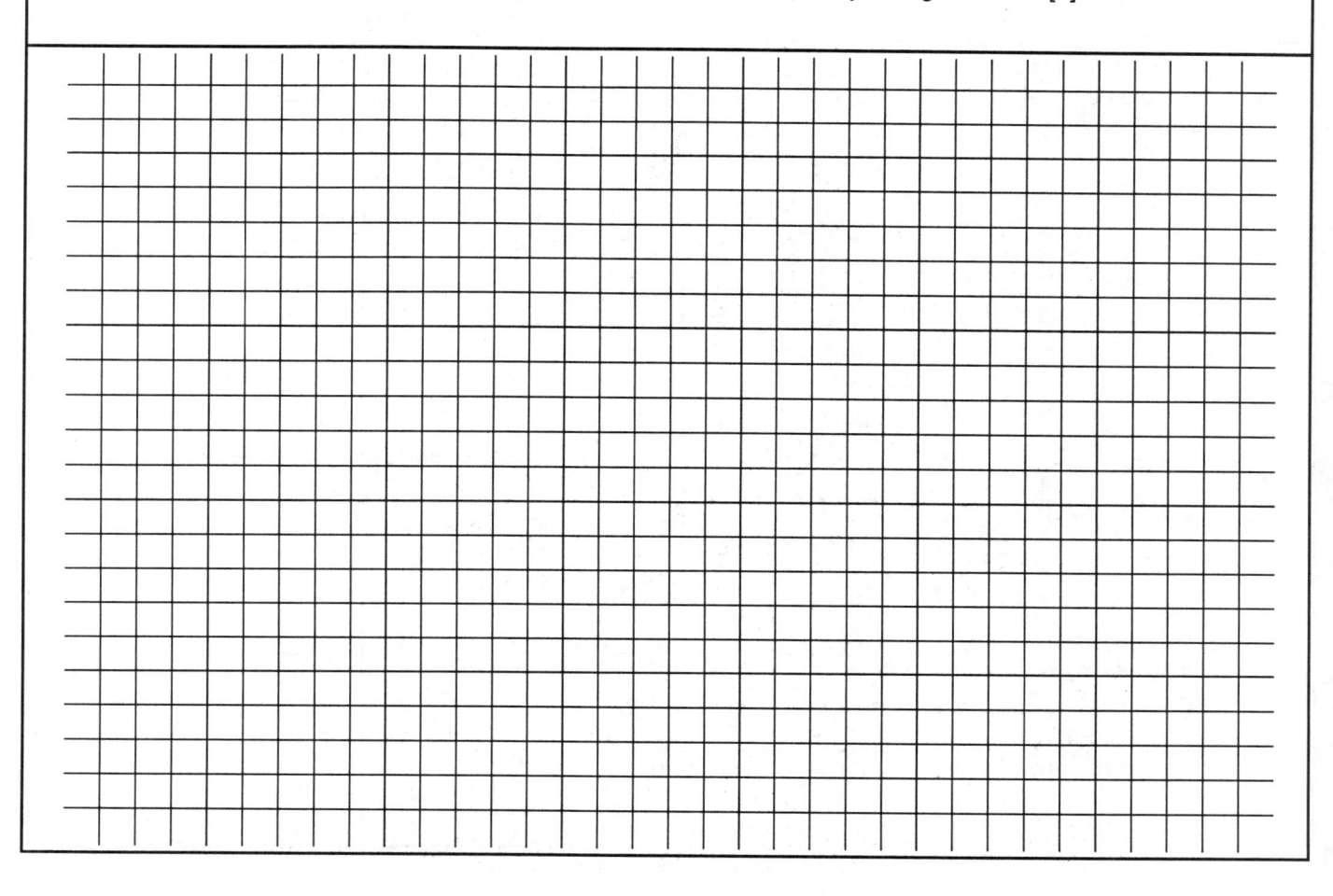

CUMULATIVE FREQUENCY HISTOGRAMS
(Continued)

4. The points scored by the A-Team in twenty basketball games are 33, 27, 24, 30, 37, 32, 35, 23, 32, 29, 26, 30, 28, 31, 29, 35, 23, 30, 25, 30.

   a. Find the mode. [2]

   b. On your answer paper, copy and complete the tables below. [2]

Interval	Tally	Frequency
35 - 37		
32 - 34		
29 - 31		
26 - 28		
23 - 25		

Interval	Cumulative Frequency
23 - 37	
23 - 34	
23 - 31	
23 - 28	
23 - 25	

   c. Construct a cumulative frequency histogram based on the table completed in part b. [4]

   d. In what interval does the median lie? [2]

5. The table below shows the distribution of scores of 20 students on a test.

Scores	Frequency
91 - 100	1
81 - 90	8
71 - 80	7
61 - 70	3
51 - 60	1

Scores	Cumulative Frequency
51 - 100	
51 - 90	
51 - 80	
51 - 70	
51 - 60	1

   a. Using the data in the Frequency column of the table, draw a frequency histogram. [4]

   b. Complete the column for Cumulative Frequency. [2]

   c. Using the data in the Cumulative Frequency column of the table, draw a cumulative frequency histogram. [4]

SEQUENTIAL MATHEMATICS
COURSE 1

WestSea Publishing Co. Inc.
(516) 420-1110 • 149 Allen Boulevard • Farmingdale, N.Y. 11735

Practice Regents Exam

Notice...
Scientific calculators must be available to all students taking this examination.

SEQUENTIAL MATHEMATICS I
Practice Regents Exam
Part I

Answer 30 questions from this part. Each correct answer will receive 2 credits. No partial credit will be allowed. Write your answers in the spaces provided on the separate answer sheet. Where applicable, answers many be left in terms of π or in radical form. [60]

1. Solve for x: $\dfrac{x}{6} = \dfrac{5}{3}$

2. Factor: $7x + 21y$

3. If two angles of a triangle measure 40 and 80, what is the number of degrees of the third angle of the triangle?

4. Solve for a: $2a + 0.6 = 10$

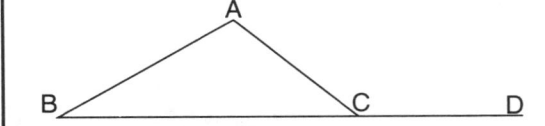

5. If (2,k) is a point on the graph of the equation $5x + 3y = 7$, what is the value of k?

6. Find the volume of a cube if the length of one edge is 6x.

7. The lengths of the sides of △ABC are 10, 24, and 26. Triangle XYZ is similar to triangle ABC. The smallest side of △XYZ is 20. Find the length of the longest side of △XYZ.

8. Let p represent "I read music" and q represent "I play in the band". Write in symbolic form using p and q: "If I do not read music, then I do not play in the band".

9. Solve the following system of equations for x.

    $x - y = 6$
    $3x + y = 14$

10. In the accompanying diagram, side $\overline{BC}$ of △ABC is extended to D and ∠ACD = 140 degrees. What is the m∠ACB in degrees?

11. In the accompanying diagram, $\overleftrightarrow{AB}$ and $\overleftrightarrow{CD}$ intersect at E, m∠AEC = 5x - 30, and m∠DEB = 3x + 10. Find the value of x.

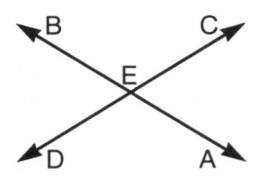

12. In a single toss of a pair of dice, what is the probability of obtaining a total count of 2?

146

SEQUENTIAL MATHEMATICS I
Practice Regents Exam

Part I (Continued)

13. In a right triangle, what is the number of degrees in the sum of the acute angles?

14. In quadrilateral ABCD, the lengths of the sides are represented by x, 4x, x + 4, and 6x - 1. Express the perimeter as a binomial in terms of x.

15. Factor: $16x^2 - 25$

16. The mean for the set of data 6, 12, x, 7 is 10. Find the value of x.

17. What is 8.5% of 200?

18. The measure of two supplementary angles are in the ratio 1:8. Find the number of degrees in the measure of the smaller angle.

19. Factor: $2x^2 + 5x - 3$

20. The test grades for a student were 75, 90, 83, 79, 83. Find the mode.

21. Solve for x: $5x - 2 < 53$

22. The lengths of two legs of a right triangle are 6 and 10. Find in radical form, the length of the hypotenuse.

Directions (23 - 35):
For each question chosen, write on the separate answer sheet the numeral preceding the word or expression that best completes the statement or answers the question.

23. Which point lies on the graph of $x + 2y = 15$?
 (1) (3,6)   (3) (10,0)
 (2) (6,3)   (4) (0,10)

SEQUENTIAL MATHEMATICS I
Practice Regents Exam

Part I (Continued)

24. The product of $7y$ and $4y^5$ is:
    (1) $11y^6$ (3) $11y^5$
    (2) $28y^6$ (4) $28y^5$

25. Which number is not a member of the solution set of $5x \geq 30$?
    (1) 11   (3) 9
    (2) 6   (4) 5

26. The expression $24y^{10} \div 6y^2$ is equivalent to:
    (1) $4y^5$ (3) $4y^8$
    (2) $18y^5$ (4) $18y^8$

27. If the radius of a circle is doubled, then the area of the circle is multiplied by:
    (1) $\frac{1}{2}$ (3) 3
    (2) 2   (4) 4

28. What is the contrapositive of the statement $p \rightarrow \sim q$?
    (1) $p \leftrightarrow \sim q$ (3) $\sim p \rightarrow q$
    (2) $\sim q \rightarrow p$ (4) $q \rightarrow \sim p$

29. The y-intercept of the graph of $y = -\frac{1}{2}x + \frac{1}{2}$ is:
    (1) $-\frac{1}{2}$ (3) -2
    (2) 2   (4) $\frac{1}{2}$

30. The value of $4!$ is:
    (1) 12   (3) $\frac{1}{4}$
    (2) 24   (4) 4

31. Which represents an irrational number?
    (1) 0   (3) 3
    (2) $\sqrt{3}$ (4) $\sqrt{25}$

32. Which inequality is represented by the graph?

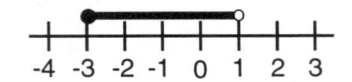

    (number line from -4 to 3 with closed dot at -3 and open dot at 1)

    (1) $-3 \leq x < 1$ (3) $-3 \leq x \leq 1$
    (2) $-3 < x \leq 1$ (4) $-3 < x < 1$

33. The expression $\sqrt{200} - \sqrt{50}$ is equivalent to:
    (1) $\sqrt{150}$ (3) $5\sqrt{2}$
    (2) $15\sqrt{2}$ (4) $2\sqrt{5}$

34. Express as a binomial: $3x(5x - 1)$
    (1) $15x^2 - 1$ (3) $3x - 15x^2$
    (2) $15x^2 - 3x$ (4) $8x^2 - 3x$

35. If a baseball team has 4 jerseys and 2 hats, how many different uniforms consisting of one jersey and one hat can be worn?
    (1) 6   (3) 8
    (2) 2   (4) 4

SEQUENTIAL MATHEMATICS I
Practice Regents Exam
Part II

Answer four question from this part. Show all work unless otherwise directed. [40]

---

36. On the same set of coordinate axes, graph the following system of inequalities and label the solution set A:

    $y + 4 > 2x$

    $y \leq -3x$

    [8,2]

37. In the accompanying diagram, ABCD is a rectangle with AB = 50 and BC = 20. The radii of circles O and P are both equal to 10. [Answer may be left in terms of π.]

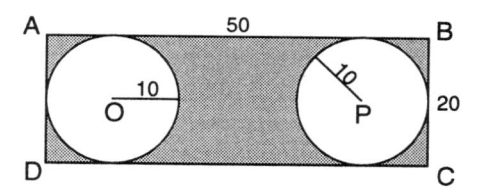

    a. What is the perimeter of ABCD? [2]
    b. What is the area of ABCD? [2]
    c. What is the circumference of circle O? [2]
    d. What is the area of circle P? [2]
    e. What is the area of the shaded region in the diagram? [2]

38. Solve the following system of equations algebraically and check:

    $3x + 2y = 19$

    $y = 4x - 7$

    [8,2]

39. Given right triangle ABC with angle C the right angle. The larger leg is 4 more than twice the smaller leg and the hypotenuse is 6 more than twice the smaller leg. Find all three sides. [Only an algebraic solution will be accepted.] [5,5]

40. The table below shows the number of families with 2, 3, 4, 5, 6 and 7 members.

No. of Members	No. of Families (frequency)
2	9
3	15
4	6
5	4
6	0
7	1

    a. On a separate piece of paper, draw a frequency histogram for the given data. [4]
    b. Find the mode. [2]
    c. What is the probability that if one family is selected, it will have three members? [2]
    d. What is the probability that if one family is selected, it will have at least 5 members? [2]

41. An eight sided polygon has the following vertices: A (-6,2), B (-2,6), C (2,6), D (6,2), E (6,-2), F (2,-6), G (-2,-6), H (-6,-2).

    a. Plot the points on a piece of graph paper. [2]
    b. Find the area of rectangle ADEH. [2]
    c. Find the area of trapezoid ABCD. [3]
    d. Find the area of the eight sided polygon ABCDEFGH. [3]

SEQUENTIAL MATHEMATICS I
Practice Regents Exam

Part II (Continued)

42. a. On a separate piece of paper, copy and complete the truth table for the statement $(\sim p \vee q) \leftrightarrow \sim(p \to \sim q)$. [8]

p	q	~p	~q	~p∨q	p→~q	~(p→~q)	(~p∨q)↔~(p→~q)
T	T						
T	F						
F	T						
F	F						

b. Write the contrapositive of the statement: [2]

"If Mary can save $2,000, then she will not need to borrow money to purchase a used automobile."

SEQUENTIAL MATHEMATICS I
Practice Regents Exam
Answer Sheet

Pupil...Teacher...

School...Grade...

Your answers to Part I should be recorded on this answer sheet.

Part I

Answer 30 questions from this part.

1	11	21	31 ....
2	12	22	32 ....
3	13	23	33 ....
4	14	24	34 ....
5	15	25	35 ....
6	16	26	
7	17	27	
8	18	28	
9	19	29	
10	20	30	

Your answers Part II should be placed on the paper provided by the school.

The declaration below should be signed when you have completed the examination.

I do hereby affirm, at the close of this examination, that I had no unlawful knowledge of the questions or answers prior to the examination, and that I have neither given nor received assistance in answering any of the questions during the examination.

_____
Signature

NOTES

NOTES